CLOUD OF
WITNESSES

The publisher acknowledges excerpt of the following material: p. xv, The Huw Morgan quotation, *How Green Was My Valley*, Robert Llewelyn, New York, Scribners, 1941; p. 5, Robert Frost, "Desert Places," in *A Further Range*, New York, Henry Holt, 1936; p. 19–20, W.H. Auden "September 1, 1939" in *Another Time*, New York, Random House, 1940; p. 40, Lawrence Binyon, "For the Fallen," in *For the Fallen & Other Poems*, London, Hodder & Stoughton, 1917.

Scripture quotations are the author's own translations from the Greek.

Copyright © 2010, Scepter Publishers, Inc.
P.O. Box 211, New York, N.Y. 10018
www.scepterpublishers.org

Printed in the United States of America

ISBN-13: 978-1-59417-088-1

CLOUD OF WITNESSES

Dead People I Knew When They Were Alive

GEORGE WILLIAM RUTLER

 Scepter

"Therefore, since we are surrounded by so great a cloud of witnesses, let us also lay aside every weight, and sin which clings so closely, and let us run with perseverance the race that is set before us." (Hebrews 12:1)

◆ ◆ ◆

CONTENTS

❧

FOREWORD

✄

The twentieth century was the American Century or more correctly that century dominated culturally, financially, and militarily by the United States. I suspect that this century too will belong to the U.S.A. but that China will be a more enduring rival than Japan or Germany or Russia. But that is another story and life is often surprising.

Pope John Paul II used to refer to New York as the capital of the world or perhaps the capital of the Western world. And so it is. We are not being untruthful or too disrespectful in pointing out that New York has the best and worst of everything.

Father Rutler is a Catholic priest in that great city and this collection of portraits constitutes an unusual book; typically so for the author's works are often unusual in their insights, their range of knowledge, and the elegance of the writing.

Catholics are now part of the North American mainstream, torn in different directions by the culture wars and with large segments seriously tempted towards liberal

Protestantism, just as many of those liberal Protestants lapse into agnosticism or morph into Evangelicals.

Father George is conservative and a Catholic from the radical center, an avowed follower and admirer of Pope John Paul II and Pope Benedict. He also belongs to that small, influential, and growing group of convert intellectuals which has enriched the Catholic community and contributed mightily to scholarship and public discourse. He deserves to rank with Cardinal Avery Dulles, S.J., Father Richard Neuhaus, and Scott Hahn.

When historians of the future will be seeking to understand better the vitality, energy, and variety of this period of history, they will be helped mightily by dipping into pot-pourri.

While Father George might not know everyone worth knowing he does introduce us to a bewildering range of characters stretching from Mother Teresa to Queen Elizabeth, the wife of George VI whom Hitler described as the most dangerous woman in Europe; from Barbara Cartland to Robert Frost, from the parish secretary to Cardinal Lustiger, Jewish archbishop of Paris and "a rabbinical clone of Wojtyla"; from a university chaplain to Billy of Engine Company 21.

We find no malice in these portraits, but he is honest, perhaps a little tougher on his fellow clerics, as he writes loyally of the humanity of his friends.

I know a few of the characters brought to life in these sketches and can vouch for their accuracy. I therefore feel confident in recommending also the larger number of personalities I did not know, captured in these vignettes, these elegant impressions of departed friends.

Father George gives us glimpses into a fascinating world, much of it conservative and Christian, not all of it grand in a secular sense, but certainly bringing us evidence of "the infinite variety of human grandeur." He is uniquely placed to reveal to us some of the persons who toiled to make the U.S.A. what it was at the zenith of its power.

GEORGE CARDINAL PELL
Archbishop of Sydney
December 16, 2009

CHARACTERS I HAVE KNOWN

※

These are the researches of Herodotus of Halicarnassus, which he publishes, in the hope of thereby preserving from decay the remembrance of what men have done and of preventing the great and wonderful actions of the Greeks and the Barbarians from losing their due meed of glory; and withal to put on record what were their grounds of feuds.

Herodotus wrote his record of human deeds five centuries before Christ, when the world already seemed weighted down with so many lives. He began his first book, *Clio*, declaring his purpose, and it has been translated many times, perhaps most floridly by Macaulay. The version above is by George Rawlinson, Camden Professor of Ancient History in the University of Oxford, whose life spanned nearly a century. When Rawlinson was born, George III and James Madison were alive, and when he died Edward VII and Theodore Roosevelt were in power. If he had not been bound by convention and the duties of his job, he might have written recollections of people he knew in those days as interesting as anything Herodotus has given us. Not just of the great names but of people who made up the rest of those days and most of whom are forgotten. No one is uninteresting, and everyone has been a character in the biography of the world.

Frail familiarity with Greek obscures a real understanding of the Greek *karakter*, which I would make the theme of the character sketches I have written. To say someone is a real character or has a lot of character or lacks character resounds with the classical sense of a *karakter* as something stamped by something outside the self. Wolves and whales have their appeal and proper dignity, but they are not great characters. The saints are the greatest characters because they are most impressionable to the divine will, and it is an indictment of our time that they are largely ignored, almost self-consciously so, by our schools. They were, as St. Catherine of Siena said, already in heaven on earth. Souls perfectly impressed by a transcendent power are perfectly unimpressed with themselves. This is the blessedness of the poor in spirit. A self so hard that it will not be impressed by timeless truths will be chiseled by mere creatures until it breaks.

I have written about characters I have known and who have impressed me because God in different ways impressed them. Perhaps most were not yet saints, and some decidedly were not so blessed and even seemed to struggle against the blessing. But each of them taught me something about the infinite variety of human grandeur. People who live lives larger than their own are living gospels written in black and white by deeds and misdeeds, and together they form a cloud of witnesses (Hebrews 12:1), stormy and serene. Some of these characters were well known, and some may be remembered only by a few. The justice without which there is no charity requires that I write only about those who have finished their earthly lives.

These are not biographies. Each gave something to me. Others could say much more about them, but by deliberately writing only vignettes, I want to make the point that some passing influence, some remark or circumstance, was personal enough to have made me something that I would not have been without them. I do not blame them if I did not learn from them all I might have or if I have failed to become what I could have become because of them. My mention of them is perhaps more like the Japanese poetry that gives an impression instead of a reproduction; but it is an impression made by that unique mystery, a human person, so important that thinkers such as Aquinas and Newman have said that it would be better for whole galaxies to collapse than one of these souls be lost. That is incomprehensible to the materialist who may not differentiate the human being from other creatures and who has difficulty conceiving of a deliberate creation at all, but it is based on an intuition common to humanity's finest hours.

While I have spent a lot of time in schools, the lives of people themselves are the best schools. When a friend asked me to coax his daughter, who had announced after her first day in kindergarten that she did not want to go back, I replied that the girl seemed to have sensed something quite right. With some rhetorical excess I said she should abandon kindergarten altogether, for it was my experience that school interrupted my education. It locks you in with your peers. That is a mistake. One's social circle should avoid one's equals. As a child I found children unexceptional and preferred the company of adults. I got to know lots of people who are dead now whom I never would have known had I waited a few years. So I have a collective memory, and oral tradition, that goes back to the eighteenth century, having spoken with people who knew people who knew people who knew people who lived then. The only real university is the universe and that is why an expression like New York University misses the point that the city is the university.

I exercised the child's father by suggesting that, instead of school, children should spend time in restaurant kitchens and shops and garages of all kinds, learning from people who actually make the world work. One day spent roaming through a real classical church building would be the equivalent of one academic term in any of our schools, and a little time spent inconspicuously in a police station would be more informative than many hours spent on social science. Formal lessons would only be required for accuracy in spelling and proficiency in public speaking, for which most public speakers in our culture are not models; and in exchange for performing some menial services, a child could learn the violin, harp, and piano from musicians in one of the better hotels or from performers in the public subways. I urged my friend to keep his child out of kindergarten because kindergarten will only lead to first grade and then the grim sequence of grade after grade begins and takes its inexorable toll on the mind born fertile but gradually numbed by the pedants who impose on the captive child the flotsam of their own infecundity.

In the case of the little girl, as in the case of all of us, she did return to school the next day, and I could only hope that in the years ahead of her she would pay attention to the faces that come her way, and listen to them speak and watch what they do, and let this become a lifelong habit. This brought to my own mind the film *How Green Was My Valley*, John Ford's 1941 version of the novel Richard Llewellyn wrote about a Welsh mining village. Walter Pidgeon starred in it with Maureen O'Hara who told me, after I had given a lecture, most interesting details about it, but nothing so charming as the words beyond charm of the character Huw Morgan looking back on his boyhood:

> I saw behind me those who had gone, and before me, those who were to come. I looked back and saw my father, and his father, and all our fathers, and in front, to see my son, and his son, and the sons upon sons beyond, and their eyes were my eyes. As I felt, so they had felt, and were to feel, as then, so now, as tomorrow and forever. Then I was not afraid, for I was in a long line that had no beginning, and no end, and the hand of his father grasped my father's hand, and his hand was in mine, and my unborn son took my right hand, and all, up and down the line that stretched from Time That Was, to Time That Is, and Is Not Yet, raised their hands to show the link, and we found that we were one, born of Woman, son of Man, made in the Image, fashioned in the Womb by the Will of God, the Eternal Father.

Caroline Irwin

❧

Call her Miss Irwin, for in the nearly ten years she was my
parish secretary I never heard anyone, save her brother,
call her Caroline. It was as if Miss was the name
bestowed with the lustral waters of the Methodist Church
whose hymnodic fellowship she left in youth to embrace
Anglicanism, which the Methodists had tried unsuccess-
fully to bring to a happier frame of mind. Agatha Christie might have formed Miss Marple fully from the brow
of Miss Irwin, like a geriatric Athena. In the films Miss
Marple was played incongruously by Gracie Fields and
unrecognizably by Margaret Rutherford, but her veritable
incarnation was Joan Hickson whom I cannot separate
from Miss Irwin.

I was a very young rector in a venerable parish of her
religion on the Main Line outside Philadelphia, and she
was more than three times my age. Miss Marple said in
several of the detective stories: The young people think
that the old people are fools, but the old people know that
the young people are fools. While Miss Irwin never patronized my occasional stabs at wisdom, I suspect that she did
not overestimate them. When I was felled in an epidemic

of pneumonia, she appeared sprightly, saying that she had
begun to feel unwell but had taken half an aspirin and
woke up refreshed. Proverbs 31:27 says the wise woman
girds her loins with strength and makes her arms strong.
Miss Irwin was like that, although she would have avoided
the oriental way of putting it.

She was born in the village where she would die, and
her house was next to the building that had supplied ice
to freshen the body of Lincoln on its funeral journey.
For counting collections, she used an abacus and dutifully
learned to use the electric adding machine I bought her,
while checking its accuracy with the old device. She spoke
English as a lady trained never to raise her voice or to let
one's spine touch the back of a chair. Though democratic
in all her ways, she took as a revelation my suggestion
that she might consult the telephone directory when the
Social Register failed her. Her love for the parish garden
was intense, and no one corrected her habit of pronounc-
ing compost as compote. In the early 1970s, when rioters
filled the streets, she continued to schedule vestry meetings
for Thursdays because for everyone that was their cook's
night out.

Having set aside religious enthusiasm, it was not her
nature to speak of prayer, but she did what she did not
speak about, and whenever we finished praying to the Eternal Light, she was the last to turn off the electric light. It
was easy to fall into the mistake of Miss Marple's nephew
who treated his dear, pretty, old fluffy Jane with an indul-
gent kindness as one who knew nothing of the world.
Miss Irwin left many well-thumbed books when she died,
and they were classics. A Ford salesman offered so kindly

to buy back her ten-year-old automobile with 1,800 miles on it. She did not sell. She once parked outside a circus pavilion and an elephant backed into her fender. Later she was stopped by a policeman who asked if she had been in a collision. When she told him that she had been struck by an elephant, she knew he wrote her off as dithery. Miss Marple thought that intuition is like reading a word without having to spell it out. Miss Irwin was intuitive. While there was never a murder in our vicarage, she solved a burglary and that was good enough.

Agatha Christie said of Miss Marple, "Though a cheerful person she always expected the worst of everyone and everything and was, with almost frightening accuracy, usually proved right." Cheerful was Miss Irwin, but she never expected the worst, though she knew that everyone could be a bit better, and she seemed to know what that bit was. She lamented an aunt who had returned from a trip to California wearing make-up, smoking, and using the expression "darn."

She dignified the title spinster, which in our day has become almost a title of denigration. St. Paul says that elderly women are not to be slanderers or slaves to drink (Titus 2:3). He would have approved of Miss Irwin. Only once did she take a sip of champagne: on the 200th birthday of the USA.

Miss Marple solved detective mysteries in her village of St. Mary Mead. In her village of Rosemont, Miss Irwin engaged another kind of mystery, The Mystery, which is not a puzzle, for the answer is provided to all those who have faith in divine providence. I hope that Miss Irwin hears a Voice now calling her, in rare fashion, "Caroline."

Robert Frost

❧

My recollections of college are inseparable from New England snow. Our songs were about the clanging bells, the crush of feet on snow and the wolf-wind wailing at the doorways. I never thought the cold too cold because I was too young for common sense about the senses. Barely had I turned sixteen when I showed up at Dartmouth. The infantile mind records some things of which it never lets go, and I have a sharp picture of hurrying in the chill past a man seventy-one years older than I, with hair like mountains of snow. "You young fellas are always in a rush." He stopped me, and that is how I first met Robert Frost. I got to know that sing-song voice and do not remember him speaking any other way.

Frost was dead two years later, and while his talks to us young fellas (college was all-male) were rare, there was a gentle hint of a world come all around to its start, for he had matriculated there; but his restless spirit had led him away in his own freshman year. Sometimes he lectured in front of a blazing hearth. He mastered the pose, and even my juvenile eye saw that there was theater in him. He combined the thespian with the Calvinist in his ambiguous line:

"Hell is a half-filled auditorium." Nor was I too young to hear in his chanting kind of reading an icy melancholy. That is how my soft soul encountered the remnants of glacial Calvinism.

Frost gleaned his precise rhythms from the Puritan instinct to be parsimonious with words. His mother had been a Swedenborgian, which I think worsened things by mixing Puritan sobriety with unresolved mysticism. "Forgive, O Lord, my little jokes on thee and I'll forgive thy great big one on me." A generation earlier that coyness had been Sturm und Drang: the background is hugeness and confusion, shading away into black and chaos. That took a toll on bucolic reverie: two daughters had nervous breakdowns and a son committed suicide.

I must say that he did not warm my New England winters, for there was a cold battle going on in him between a benevolent and even elegant God and the God of arbitrary anger and unmerited predestinations. This was his lover's quarrel with the world. His long-dead wife, Elinor, thought that he shared her atheism. Not so. But it was distressfully not so:

> They cannot scare me with their empty spaces
> Between stars on stars where no human race is.
> I have it in me so much nearer home
> To scare myself with my own desert places.

He was shaped by the anthropomorphism of George Santayana and the pragmatism of William James, but that seemed only to embitter him in his inability to reconcile the light and dark places. His definitive poem, *Stopping by Woods on a Snowy Evening*, is as shocking in its casualness

about fear as Goya is in his violence. The grandfatherly
benignity that he affected toward the end, as he shuffled
and I skipped across the college green, was a calculus of
charity in the face of all these deep questions about God
that had no resolution in the flinty recesses of a Yankee
mind. The only poem of his I knew pretty well was *The
Road Not Taken* of 1916, and when my freshman gauche-
ness asked what the fork in that road really was, he replied:
"The fork in the road just south of Thetford Junction."

It would be a stretch to put Robert Frost in the front
row of the great cloud of witnesses, but after reading St.
Thomas Aquinas on the Holy Ghost, which he could
handle as a lifelong Latinist, he wrote: "You know my mild
prejudice against Ghost Writers. But I am sublimated out
of my shoes by the thought that in Heaven we will all be
Ghost Writers if we write at all. Maybe we won't write any
more than we marry there. Everything will be done out of
wedlock and said off the record."

I do not think an atheist would have disdained free
verse as a blasphemy. He said that when Jehovah revealed
himself as I AM, it was as a command to write in iambics
and not in free verse, and I suspect that is also why he
told a rabbi friend that irreligion is worse than atheism.
Though he might have found chaos more explicable, a
sense of order in the universe raised his wrestling notions
of a Calvinist God and a Catholic God to a bleak level of
pain. But it may have been a redemptive pain. He freely
wrote things out for me, but one day when I asked him to
inscribe a Bible he said, "No. I didn't write it."

Florence Dermot Cohalan

❦

"**Y**ou will make an excellent wife and mother," replied the handwriting expert when Monsignor Florence Daniel Cohalan responded to a newspaper advertisement for free analysis of signatures. His penmanship would require a Rosetta Stone for deciphering, but the confusion arose because Florence had been named for the Saint Abbot of Bangor in County Down. His own family, with tradition of service under Lafayette in the American Revolution, had come from County Cork. From her house, an aunt watched the Lusitania sink. From his grandmothers house, DeValera watched Michael Collins drive by just before his assassination. Thereafter he esteemed only Collins. Daniel, his father, and two uncles were judges of the New York State Supreme Court at the same time, and Daniel came to be the leading voice of the Irish in the city of New York. In 1917, Arthur Brisbane wrote, "Powerful in intellect and of inflexible integrity, Cohalan stands out as one of the great Americans of our time." Woodrow Wilson did not think so and vowed never to shake his hand.

Florence was born in 1907. His mother sang "Danny Boy" to his father the night before she died in childbirth, and he was reared by a stepmother. A weak heart invalided him as a child, and he never ate a vegetable, nor did he exercise (save for riding in Ireland in summers and walking trips with Churchill's cousin, Sir Shane Leslie). Chief Justice Charles Evans Hughes vainly gave him golf clubs when he was a teenager in the vain hope that it would interest him in the outdoors. Victor Herbert named his operetta *Aileen* for Florence's sister, who became a Madame of the Sacred Heart and died at 100. Doomed to an early grave, he lived ninety-three years and outlived all his classmates from Georgetown, Harvard, and Dunwoodie Seminary.

When ordained, his wide associations with burnished figures of a gilded age discomfited a narrow clerical establishment. He spent most of his life teaching history to hundreds of minor seminarians and then was pastor of a small parish on Staten Island. His official history of the Archdiocese of New York, a model of erudition and charitable judgment, could have been followed by a longer one about the whimsies and gossip that pump the blood of culture. Total recall of the tables of royal European consanguinity and affinity accompanied knowledge of which nineteenth-century archbishops wore toupees. Impeccable in his duties to the Breviary and altar, he sheltered no extravagant piety and claimed that while it would be fine to be found dead slumped over a prie-dieu, friends would assume he had a premonition.

He never taught me in a classroom, but more than fifteen years of rectory table conversation made him my most influential teacher. Once a callow curate whose social analysis reeked of the trends of the 1970s stopped by for dinner and fled as soon as he could after our conversation on the Merovingian kings, Marshal Petain, and Anastasia Romanov. "Please, one conversation at a time," he often said, and all knew whose conversation it would be. When I nudged him from what seemed to be a comatose state, he stared and said: "I was just thinking—since Borromeo himself, until Pius VII appointed Consalvi, probably the greatest diplomat was Flavio Chigi under Alexander VII."

The Cohalan library was breathtaking, and when his sight went, he uncomplainingly submitted to readers or listened exclusively to Mozart, who has no equal. A policeman searching the rectory for a burglar got a discourse on Arthur Conan Doyle. Young and old made him their confessor, while he beckoned people whose personalities had irregular corners. He had sailed with the murderer Harry K. Thaw and enjoyed dear friends who well into the 1950s dressed in turn-of-the-century clothing and every year in Paris took long detours in their ancient touring car to avoid an avenue named for Franklin Roosevelt. He lent a sympathetic ear to a professor whose unrelieved grief at the death of his wife found expression in wearing her dresses and wig. The man "does have his little ways." To those most likely to disapprove, he would announce his plans for a Confraternity of Catholic Executioners. He changed with good changes and lamented changes that were not good. Reverent to those whom an inscrutable providence had designated his superiors, the eye of the historian detected in Paul VI some similarities to Clement XIV.

He hoped there would be an alcove in heaven where the popes compare the vicissitudes of their reigns. He would be a prime man to refresh their memories. Lord Acton called religion the key of history. Monsignor Cohalan unlocked whole centuries with that key. Shortly before he was called on high, he said to me, "I know I talk a lot, but I also listen a lot."

Cuthbert Aikman Simpson

✣

"What would you do if Henry VIII stepped out of that frame?" asked King Edward VII of his friend Herbert Vaughan, S.J., in the royal picture gallery. Father Vaughan paused not: "I would ask the ladies to leave the room." A portrait of Cuthbert Aikman Simpson by Graham Sutherland, with his mortarboard and inseparable cigarette, now hangs next to Henry VIII in the Christ Church dining hall in Oxford, where Simpson was the Very Reverend dean from 1959 to 1969. He was not a Jesuit like Vaughan, and he was a Catholic only as an Anglican might suppose himself to be. Foxes *Book of Martyrs* in 1563 depicted a Protestant Cuthbert Simpson being racked in the Tower, and the parish records of Egton in York list a Cuthbert Simpson as a Catholic recusant under Charles I. While my Cuthbert inherited that braided tradition, he could not easily have passed as rackable by Queen Mary. He authored with a friend of mine a manual on the proper ceremonials of the Mass that was almost Tridentine. Once he complimented another friend of mine on his aesthetic ringing of the Sanctus bell.

For years he had brilliantly taught Hebrew in New
York. To have an American, that is one born in Canada
on Prince Edward Island, appointed to the vaunted office
of dean of Christ Church was a radical thing at the time.
This physical composite of Spencer Tracy and Basil Rath-
bone had a magnificent temper, once having tossed a student down his front steps in a conversation about Senator
McCarthy. A Manhattan conductor evicted him from a
public bus for bad language. When an Oxford freshman
asked him if he knew Hebrew, he shouted, "I am the
@%#! Regius Professor of Hebrew!" Simpson's books
on revelation in the Old Testament and the pre-Deutero-
nomic narrative of the Hexateuch leave anything similar in
the dust. In the revolutionary years of the late 1960s, his
successful method for quelling student demonstrators was
to invite any budding Bolshevik in for a stiff martini. On
Sundays, his verger carrying a silver mace led him along the
Tom Quad to his waiting cocktail, Simpson in his scarlet
academic robes, silk stockings, and silver-buckled shoes.

When the cathedral organist gave him a long melody
to intone the Gloria, his voice rang throughout the choir:
"Does that man think I am a *%#?@! canary?" In 1965,
William Walton dedicated his anthem "The Twelve" to the
dean, and on the day that he landed on the college grounds
by helicopter, the attendant choirboys sang, "Lo, he comes
with clouds descending," the words of which were written by an alumnus, Charles Wesley. At the shallow age of
twenty-two, I had the temerity to ask him if he had considered moving the altar and celebrating facing the people.
This was during a luncheon, just the two of us alone, in
the deanery dining room where King Charles I had lived

during the Civil War. The dean growled in prophetic tones, "Tell me why liturgists are the only modern creatures who consider the word primitive to be something good?" The bones of St. Frideswide by the altar shook and the ghost of King Charles hummed in assent.

His son had been killed in the Second World War, and each year when he lectured on David's lament for his fallen son, the tears of a great man flowed down his craggy face as he intoned, "O my son Absalom, my son, my son Absalom!" (2 Samuel 19:33). It requires liberties to suggest that he would have become a Catholic of the Petrine obedience had he lived longer, but he surely would have uttered the outcries of the Judges of Israel had he lived to see the shambles and perversity of the ecclesiastical institution he served. The rising starlet Hans Küng told the cosmic meteor Cuthbert that Vatican II had ushered in a new regard for Scriptures that would heal the Protestant wounds. The dean replied as if casually flicking dandruff, "Good luck to you! We Protestants have been arguing for 400 years as to what are the agreed results of the Holy Ghost."

Not bereft of humor, he assigned me to accompany a grand lady in her bright yellow Daimler on a search for a Georgian silver salt cellar. And not bereft of humility, he fell to his knees at a garden party to show me the little blue door in his garden wall that was Lewis Carroll's entrance to Wonderland. He lies buried on the other side of the door. His elegant portrait remains hard by pompous Henry VIII, and I have often thought that were the king to step out of his frame, like a Gilbert and Sullivan ghost in *Ruddigore*, the dean would tell the king to go back.

Elizabeth Pike

❧

M y grandmother spoke of Cousin Lizzie often and received letters from her hometown of Macclesfield, a Cheshire town in England, all the long distance to New Jersey. That was when the Atlantic Pond was the length of a galaxy. I was barely voting age when I met Cousin Lizzie in 1967. She was older and grander than Grandma had described and so simply nice that I have decided simple niceness may be a radiant grace.

Elizabeth Pike harbored tales of my maternal family, way back to the olden times before Robin Hood haunted Sherwood Forest. Cousin Lizzie had various recollections of Capesthorne, the great hall rebuilt in a frenzy of Jacobean sturdiness. By a remarkable coincidence, the late twentieth-century chatelaine of Capesthorne, Lady Bromley-Davenport, had grown up in my old Pennsylvania parish. Her husband was a favorite of the British tabloids for his convinced belief in ghosts. Cousin Lizzie knew many stories of ancestors whose lives had been intertwined with that massive pile; some had reason to be agitated beyond the grave. Lady Bromley-Davenport once showed my visiting parents a museum of American furniture she had installed to let the British know that Americans could do Chippendale better.

Two of my grandmother's brothers, cousins of Cousin Lizzie, were killed in the Ypres Salient during World War I. Grandma kept a stiff upper lip about it, but she also kept their Bibles and *Dulce et decorum est* memorial cards. The redcoated 22nd (Cheshire) Regiment, to which my grandfather belonged in the final years of Queen Victoria, had fought with Wolfe in Quebec and with Napier in India. It is possible that one of my ancestors ordered to Massachusetts by George III shot at the man who fired the shot heard 'round the world at Lexington.

Cousin Lizzie's baronial tales of these things were told by the fire in her little cottage. She was born when Gladstone had just succeeded Disraeli, and I had a sense of rare privilege in speaking to a true Victorian for whom things Edwardian were louche and innovative. Blithe as she was about the bad behavior of the landed gentry—not to mention William IV, who supposedly dishonored a forebear— she was reticent about one enormous detail: Antecedents had succumbed to the preaching of John Wesley in Macclesfield, and she had married in "chapel" rather than in the Established Church.

Her gentle confession of this opened an entire age of church squabbles, as she added that my grandparents' marriage had been inked in the proper parish register. In that parish church of St. Michael, founded by Queen Eleanor in 1278, is the tomb of a knight of Agincourt and a tablet with the names of my great-uncles and a painfully long number of combatants going back centuries but virtually exploding in the horrific time of the Great War.

Cousin Lizzie was childless, and her shining kindness grew ancient as she outlived most of her family. On her upright piano was a photograph of two little boys, one black and one white, at a keyboard. I am not certain that she ever met anyone black. With the unaffected *gravitas* of Solon, she told me—in that time of racial conflagration in America—that harmony requires both black and white keys. This was the insight of a dear lady whose own grandfather had raised the flag against the Baluchis at Scinde. Only once did she commit a self-reference. When the Second World War contradicted the promise that the Great War was the War to End All Wars, she took in a Jewish boy refugee from eastern Europe. He was the son she never had, and when peace came, he went. Years later, a Rolls Royce arrived outside Cousin Lizzie's cottage. Her little Jewish boy had "done well for himself" in London and came to thank her with the gift of a fur coat. She never wore the mantle of gratitude, simply because she had no occasion to wear it, but how proud she was that her child had been so good.

My grandmother told me that there were 108 steps from the railway station to the church. When I arrived, I counted the steps, and when I reached the 108th, the bells of St. Michael's pealed. As it was not on the hour, the change ringers may have been rehearsing. Or perhaps my great-uncles enshrined in the church, and all their family back to Norman times, had been stirred by the approach of kin. Cousin Lizzie and her tribe with an ear for Wesley had been stretching to hear peals from Galilee, and one hopes that on the other side of the bells she finds a quality of glory that is positively nice.

W. H. Auden

❧

Delusion thinks that the self is a steady axle, and everyone else spins about in the turmoil of change and its toll on the flesh. W. H. Auden was only a few years older than I am now when, in my early 20s, he seemed to me half as old as time. His face was so wrinkled; I had never seen anything like it. I had seen weather-beaten faces, blown red and scuffed by gales and wars, but I had never seen so many wrinkles. A friend of his from schoolboy days remarked that it seemed to have come on all of a sudden.

It also struck me as rare and quite noble that so English an Englishman should have such a love for New York: not the anthropological curiosity and patronizing romanticism many of his countrymen have for the city, but an outright love for it. He lived here long enough and was often back and forth when not living here. Through friends he came to me, and I knew so little about him that he found my ignorance relaxing. On the few occasions we discussed much, it was never of literature, although he had sharp views on Prayer Book revision. He was prescient in the damage that changes to the texts would do to the English church of his allegiance. It had gone so far that he was muttering about becoming Russian Orthodox. Romanism would be too much of a surrender. He particularly objected to changing the Holy Ghost to Holy Spirit because, he fragilely argued, whiskey is a spirit, too.

Of whiskey he had come to know quantities, and on one occasion, I had to help him into a taxi when he was on the verge of passing out. I had not known anyone that far gone, and I recall the straining dignity with which he conducted himself in an awkward condition. Only later did I learn of his multiple sadnesses and moral ambiguities, but not once in our company did his demons make him say or do anything beneath the holiness that he deeply wanted. He was a studied actor and enjoyed the part he marked out for himself. I have never been able to play "background music" since the time he came in carpet slippers to a black-tie sherry party I gave for him and bellowed over my Victrola: "Do you want to listen to me or to that?"

Unlike many actors on the shaky stage of culture in the 1960s, he knew that no drama matches the eternal drama of Redemption. He wrote:

> Just as we were all, potentially, in Adam when he fell, so we were all, potentially, in Jerusalem on that first Good Friday before there was an Easter, a Pentecost, a Christian, or a Church. . . . Few are important enough to imagine being Pilate or good enough churchmen to suppose we might have been of the Sanhedrin. In my most optimistic mood I see myself as a Hellenized Jew from Alexandria visiting an intellectual friend. We are walking along, engaged in philosophical argument. Our path takes us past the base of Golgotha. Looking up, we see

an all too familiar sight—three crosses surrounded by a
jeering crowd. Frowning with prim distaste, I say, "It's
disgusting the way the mob enjoy such things. Why can't
the authorities execute criminals humanely and in private by giving them hemlock to drink, as they did with
Socrates?" Then, averting my eyes from the disagreeable
spectacle, I resume our fascinating discussion about the
nature of the True, the Good, and the Beautiful.

I take those lines as an indictment of myself, for all the
while that I was prodding Auden for something shining
to say about the True, the Good, and the Beautiful, that
wrinkled face was engraved with intimations of the Father
and the Son and the Holy Spirit, and I in my young clum-
siness with deep things just kept pouring him some lesser
spirit on ice. He had lived long enough in New York to
require ice with his whiskey.

Auden admired Kierkegaard for making Christianity
seem Bohemian. He was looking in a mirror. His Oxford
College finally agreed to place a small portrait of him in
its great hall, but in the most Bohemian corner next to the
kitchen. Much of him still is in New York, and when the
smoke was twirling so cruelly above the city in the days
after September 11, 2001, there were those who remembered verses some veiled prophet inspired him to write in
1939: "The unmentionable odour of death / Offends the
September night."

Josephine Cullen

꒰❀꒱

hen I was a curate in our Wall Street parish, Josephine Cullen was the housekeeper. After more than thirty years working there, she moved uptown to the same job in the Church of Our Saviour, where I sometimes visited her for tea, her Celtic penicillin that sustained her until her death in 2003. Neither of us had any notion that soon I would be appointed pastor of that parish.

Josephine had come from Ireland in the 1940s and gone to work in the new church built on historic Cedar and William Streets for the financial district. She dutifully made the long descent from the rectory above the church to answer the doorbell as it frequently was rung by ragged men hoping for a sandwich.

On a day when the bell had rung too often, she barked an unfeeling greeting on the primitive intercom and was told, "This is Cardinal Spellman." She was not easily fooled. Voices, sometimes slurred, had identified themselves as presidents and archangels. "You tramp. If you're the Cardinal, you should be speaking to the Monsignor." So Monsignor Piggott took charge and soon enough told Josephine that it was indeed himself. His Eminence was

admitted, with an Italian clergyman, as Josephine withdrew to her room. The Cardinal asked for her, who knelt
and kissed his ring. "Are you the young lady who called me
a tramp? I have been called far worse." He then introduced
Monsignor Montini, who wanted to see the fine new
church that was a war memorial. That a future pope had
stood in her kitchen was ever after invoked as just cause
not to replace the cracking linoleum.

Like many of her race, she was not silent on matters
of significance or insignificance, nor was she incapable
of spinning her syntax into fine symmetries of speech.
Frustrated with the unkempt condition of my desk, she
declared with affected resignation that the only difference between my sitting room and the Titanic was that
they had a band. She was unusual among her peers in
holding the political Kennedy family in contempt, and
she even forced me once into an uncharacteristic posture
of defending Senator Edward Kennedy when she ascribed
the various orthopedic problems in his family to the life
they led.

In this and in many other ways she was of a highly
original mind, and while her tendency to detect a cloud
around every silver lining inoculated her against enthusiasm, much of her outward sullenness was calculated for
effect. It cannot be said that she seduced others by her
culinary adventures; her favorite cheese was processed,
and the rest of the menu ran from A to B. Nor was her
dining room Baroque: its principal decoration was a pair
of wooden salt and pepper shakers labeled Souvenir of
Miami. An Advent wreath of undying plastic lay mourn-
fully forty-eight weeks of the year in front of a notice that

said Jesus Unseen was listening to every table conversation. Josephine had excellent hearing, too.

Modern replacements for the thinning ranks of old-style rectory housekeepers cannot match the gentle pride, one Rosary from snobbery, with which Josephine never served the household of less than a Domestic Prelate. The virtuous woman is not afraid of the snow, for all her household are clothed with scarlet (Proverbs 31:21), and for Josephine that was a monsignorial color. This did not detach her from the more soberly dressed curates to whom she was balm when they shared with her a grievance.

Josephine kept a long list of intentions and told her beads with the same dispatch with which she cleaned house. Not given to piety of the sentimental schools, she let her feelings be known loudly and broadly when a Filipino woman of far distant piety removed a finger from the Lourdes statue that Josephine had donated.

There is an oral tradition of a housekeeper in a venerable Manhattan parish who parted the velvet curtains behind the altar early one morning and announced to the sparse faithful: "There will be no Mass this morning. The pastor is not feeling so fine. And as a matter of fact, I'm not feeling so fine myself." She then bowed and withdrew, slowly closing the curtains like Sarah Bernhardt dying in Cleopatra. On earth such women never were paid the price above rubies that Sacred Scripture calculates them to be, but if they were like Josephine, they had their consolations. An instinctive pessimism, rooted in the tests of a toilsome reality, may see with surprise at the Great Assize that higher clouds do indeed have silver linings, and among them it is easy to think that Josephine will not be out of place.

Edward Piszek

❧

Having known Edward Piszek for nearly fifteen years, I still consider my mistaking him for the grounds-keeper of the Colorado retreat house where we first met understandable. He stood apart from the rest of my audience, arranging folding chairs in a work shirt and overalls. He had noticed that someone needed help and he helped. That is what he did all his life until he died of bone cancer in March 2004 at the age of eighty-seven.

Familiarity with hard work came from his parents, who had immigrated to Philadelphia from Poland. Getting punched up by neighborhood boys who raucously slurred such foreigners did not make him a zealot, nor did he lick his wounds. In lean years he helped to sell his mother's fish sticks door-to-door, and eventually her recipe and his business acumen turned a $350 investment in 1946 into Mrs. Paul's Kitchens, Inc., which he sold in 1982 when it had annual sales of $100 million.

Poland scarcely concerned him until a representative of CARE asked him to donate an ambulance for that distressed land. From then, Ed turned his very American eyes to his ancestral homeland, where in the 1950s and 1960s

tuberculosis was widespread. He battled the Communist
bureaucrats and donated a whole fleet of ambulances,
X-ray machines, and examination centers, performing
his works with practical anonymity. Years later, a medical
intern taking a delegation of Westerners through an abandoned TB ward told them, "The story is that an American
came over and cured it. But it was a long time ago. Now
TB is something we hardly think about."

Conscious of what he considered a limited formal
education, he put his brains to work in educating Americans about Polish culture through his Project Pole and the
Copernicus Society and donated the Philadelphia house
of Tadeusz Kosciuszko to the National Park Service. He
started the Peace Corps Partners in Teaching English
because he said he was not eloquent himself but was sure
that democracy would grow in former Communist countries if people knew the language of democracy. In the
same vein, he was able to establish the European center
for the Little League in the town of Kutno to form children in the sportsmanship and self-respect that Marxism
had drained from their schools, and he deliberately named
it the Little League Baseball Leadership Training Center.
During the Solidarity strikes, Ed sustained the workers
with millions of pounds of frozen fish that he was able
to get to them *magna cum difficultate*. And he airlifted food
to Ukraine after the Chernobyl disaster.

An abiding friendship with John Paul II began when the
pope was archbishop of Krakow. With palpable glee and a
sense of intrigue he told me in hushed tones how in Communist times he had outfitted a car with a typewriter so
that Wojtyla could compose and dictate while being driven

about, since the episcopal palace may have been bugged. He consoled by telephone his other close friend, Lech Walesa, after his electoral defeat. Ed had warned him during the election that his people would turn him out just as Churchill had been turned out after the war. An incredulous Walesa had been confident of victory. Ed said to me, "I was right."

Three things made him veritably sparkle. One was the Peace Corps language project. Another was his longstanding friendship with James Michener, who was as literary as Ed was not. Michener saw the man in Piszek and one got the impression that he learned more from Ed than Ed learned from him. He was docile to Ed's persuasion and finally agreed to write the novel *Poland*, which became one of his top best-sellers. A third delight to him, which engendered a classical pride of piety like the old Romans at their ancestral altars, was the purchase of George Washington's headquarters outside Philadelphia in Fort Washington, Emlen House. Ed was an American after all, and he died as a father surrounded by his children in the house of the Father of the Country.

The boy who sold his mother's fish helped to wipe out diseases and bring down an empire that he knew was genuinely evil. He helped a relatively obscure clergyman who became a pope. As at our first meeting, Ed always blended into the wallpaper unnoticed, but he was holding up the wall. In a world of many who wear their achievements heavily, he shrugged his off with a lightness lifted by the graces of many confessions and communions. When informed that George Washington had quietly gone back to his plantation after the Revolution, King George III, the farmer king, called him the most distinguished man living. George Washington and Ed Piszek rightly lived in the same house.

G. E. M. Anscombe

✣

For Ludwig Wittgenstein, whose student and literary executor Gertrude Elizabeth Margaret Anscombe had been, philosophy is not a thing but an action, rather as Plato called it the highest form of music. Elizabeth Anscombe acted upon that, moving from the utilitarian and Kantian concepts of ethics rooted in obligation to a revival of Aristotelian virtue ethics. She may have been the greatest of twentieth-century analytic philosophers, a claim staked in her treatise *Intention* in 1957. One cannot imagine Karol Wojtyla writing *The Acting Person* without it. A bishop and a professor told me that in separate audiences the first thing John Paul II said when they mentioned Oxford was: "Do you know Professor Anscombe?"

She lived eighty-one years, reciting the sorrowful mysteries of the Rosary as she died surrounded by her husband, the philosopher Peter Geach, and four of her seven children. From 1970 until her retirement in 1986 she held the chair at Cambridge University first held by Wittgenstein. When she confounded C. S. Lewis in a response at the Oxford Socratic Society on February 2, 1948, he never attempted theology again, except to alter the third chapter of his *Miracles*. She was surprised and edified that he was so abashed, and their bond was unbroken.

A. J. Ayer once told her: "If you didn't talk so slowly, people wouldn't think you were so profound." Elizabeth talked slowly in part because she was constantly drawing on cigars, blowing smoke rings like the caterpillar in Wonderland before making a pronouncement. Entering a Cambridge common room, she was bemused to hear some earnest women arguing that nothing in the Bible prevented the ordination of women. She calmly leaned her rather comfortable flesh against the mantelpiece, adjusted her monocle, recited the names of the Twelve Apostles, and blew a smoke ring at them. I have that story from my own tutor who later, of a different mind, went on to become archbishop of Canterbury.

She was too Catholic to be patient with third-rate feminism, outward appearance notwithstanding. Elizabeth always wore trousers. Entering the apostolic palace to see the pope, she approached the gate in trousers and pulled a string, lowering her skirt like a parachute. Her last conscious act on her deathbed was to kiss her husband, but she abjured her married name. Telephoning her in Cambridge from Oxford, which is possibly the world's longest long-distance call, I asked to speak with Mrs. Geach. "There is no such person," said the voice before hanging up. A second call to Professor Anscombe initiated a friendly conversation with no allusion to the faux-pas. She had been diligent in securing an academic posting for me in Oxford, but she could also be absent-minded. Her young children wandered along the canal with signs pinned to them: "Do not feed me, I am a Geach." She was, nevertheless, an utterly devoted mother.

As a maelstrom of dissent swirled around the publication of *Humanae Vitae*, she and her husband toasted it with champagne. I rather thought her brilliant essays on abortion were academic exercises until she was dragged into court for demonstrating outside an abortion mill. A picture of her standing before the judge, with Professor John Finnis as her barrister, should be painted as an icon for the coming generation. While she was not a Wittgensteinian, she vigorously lived out truth as an action. St. Dionysius thought of history as philosophy teaching by example. Elizabeth Anscombe is now an ageless historical figure, and I think she sensed that possibility as a delightful curiosity, the way she came to reconsider St. Anselm as the sort of fellow whose greatness makes him a constant companion.

Barbara Cartland

❧

"The less women fuss about themselves, the less they talk to other women, the more they try to please their husbands, the happier the marriage is going to be." The audacious femininity of Dame Barbara Cartland (1901–2000) was more radically feminist than the feminists she infuriated. She ran cosmetics and health food corporations (honey was her secret to living ninety-eight vigorous years, and she never failed to take two brandies and soda at meals). The first white woman to enter King Tut's tomb, she patented the turquoise shade she found there for eye shadow.

The Guinness Book of World Records lists her second only to God and first among human authors in the number of books sold: more than one billion, 700 titles in thirty-six languages, mostly romance novels evocative and even provocative but decent. A historical romance is the only kind of book where chastity really counts. She prayed before dictation, but her cosmology was vague: "As long as the plots keep arriving from outer space, I'll go on with my virgins." Basil Cardinal Hume decided not to write an introduction to her book of spiritual thoughts because of her belief in Martians.

We became friends when I was filming a documentary in London. She liked lunching at Claridges every week with Lord Mountbatten, whose photograph with her she left me. "I have sat at this table every Wednesday since 1917," she announced. Once she produced a handwritten letter from the Queen Mother, who had been trout-fishing at her Castle of May in Scotland, a theatrical way of assuring me that if Her Majesty was *compos mentis*, so could a grande dame one year younger be. Relations were strained with her step-granddaughter, the Princess of Wales, though vivid enough for her to propose that I catechize Diana the following summer, but that was the fatal summer. She was sure that the princess, muddled in ways, wanted to act on promptings of Mother Teresa.

Dame Barbara knew that one can hardly be more lapsed than to have lapsed from the Church of England, as she threatened to do. "I know you don't think our bishops are real bishops, but at least they used to be gentlemen and now they are not even that." Her beloved mother Polly, who sedately died behind the wheel of her stationary Rolls Royce at 100, had climbed up the Holy Stairs in Rome on her knees, declared at the top that the pope was right, and converted.

Philanthropies included housing for the aged and civil rights reform for Romany Gypsies who made the Queen of Romance an honorary Gypsy queen. She confided that when she turned eighty she had to choose between preserving her figure or her face, and she chose the face. What did I think? The imperious question was hard to answer as she wore theatrical makeup in the daylight. "I loathe dressing like this, but the people expect it." Whenever she arrived all

pink and feathered in a huge touring car with lap dogs and
a Rudolph Valentino clone as chauffeur, it was easy to forget that Winston Churchill had written the preface to her
biography of her brother Ronald, who died with another
brother, Arthur, at Dunkirk.

She became something of a surrogate grandmother but
was too coquettish for that title and did not blink when a
tabloid reporter tried to make us an item. Camfield Place,
her country house, had belonged to Beatrix Potter. For my
father in his last years, she sent a recording of herself singing "A Nightingale Sang in Berkeley Square." Papa's criti-
cism of her voice meant that he actually enjoyed it. When
my father died, she sent my mother a gilded leaf from a
tree planted by Elizabeth I. She is buried next to that tree
in an environmentally friendly cardboard coffin.

Gerald Leslie Brockhurst

❦

In 1940 four French teenaged boys followed a dog into
the cave of Lascaux and discovered nearly 600 sophis-
ticated paintings and 1,500 engravings almost 17,000
years old. These paintings and engravings moved the
elegantly stubborn soul of Andre Malraux to factor the
possibility of a higher hand in the human condition. My
first confrontation with the soul splashed into paint was
far from Paleolithic. I was ten. My father had already made
me an easel when the painting urge first hit me.

As Gerald Leslie Brockhurst was born in 1890 and
died in 1978, he was sixty-five when I knocked on his door
in Franklin Lakes, New Jersey. It was a sunny afternoon,
and it had to be Sunday because our family ritual was to
drive about the country roads in the two-tone Chevrolet
Bel Air station wagon after church and the big Sunday dinner, listening to the canary trilling on the radio's "Hartz
Mountain Hour." A child's ear thought that the bird had
actually mastered Franz Lehar and Victor Herbert.

The For Sale sign was a magnet to my parents, who
were looking to buy. The vastness of the white Georgian-
style mansion meant that we would not buy it, but my

father was not averse to adventure. In no time we were in the cool halls of my first artistic hero. He seemed charmed that I had no idea who he was and showed me a chest from the Armada, and I have every reason to believe it was so. With dramatic flourish he pointed to a sealed lead box in it that he had never opened and which prompted a homily on the vanity of this world's trinkets.

He had lived in the years of the First World War in Ireland with his wife Anais, having gone on from the Birmingham School of Art to garner all the medals at the Royal Academy. There he met Augustus John, whose portrait of Rev. Martin D'Arcy, S.J., is to me a high-water mark in the tiny circle of significant modern clerical portraiture. He branched out to etchings and printmaking, and his 1932 etching "Adolescence" of a nude reflected in her mirror is one of the modern masterpieces of the genre. Brockhurst's model was the teenaged Dorette Woodward, whom he later married, and who figured along with his sister-in-law in a scandalous divorce case that thrilled the haut-monde.

Fleeing the old world in 1939, his sensibilities led him to a leafy estate in New Jersey, where folks like my family had no idea that the woman who never appeared during our visits had rattled many cages in Europe. My father only raised an eyebrow when Brockhurst told of Hitler sitting for his portrait. My mother was just slightly less approving that he had painted the Duchess of Windsor. When that picture was auctioned at Sothebys in 1998 it brought a huge six-figure bid. My mother would not have given a penny for it. The Brockhurst manner was influenced by Piero della Francesca and Leonardo, but with a coolness closer to Botticelli. The result was a contrarian style

that critics said placed appearance above character. In the
instance of Hitler and Mrs. Simpson, that did not hurt.
He also brushed John Paul Getty and Marlene Dietrich as
a society artist, and as such there is no faster shooting star
in the artistic firmament. But the same was said of Sargent
and de Laszlo, so we can wait and see.

As for the ladies in his life, the defense could subpoena
painters from Caravaggio to Delacroix to Picasso. If he
has any place in the Cloud of Witnesses (he never breathed
a word of religion in my presence), it may be through the
intercession of Leonardo himself, whose last words were: "I
have offended God and mankind because my work did not
reach the quality it should have." I attest this: In Franklin
Lakes, New Jersey, that silken salonist opened to a young
boy sights as holy and strange as the bulls and ibexes that
prehistoric souls painted in the cave of Lascaux.

Blessed Mother Teresa

❧

I n the 1935 film *The Crusades*, there is a breathless moment when Loretta Young pleads with Henry Wilcoxon, playing Richard the Lion Heart, "You gotta save Christianity, Richard! You gotta!" Though not a high point in cinematic art, the line reminds me of how so many spoke to Mother Teresa, now Blessed. All who knew her have their stories to tell, but common to most encounters with her was a confidence that she could do something about the fragile circumstance that believers and half-believers found themselves in at the end of the millennium.

Strange to say, I cannot remember our first meeting, which was in 1980 when I was studying in Rome. In the moral constancy of her presence, every conversation seemed the same and the surroundings were totally irrelevant. But she always gave the impression that she had all the time in the world, and the one to whom she was speaking was the only other one in that world. Once I arrived at the ancient church of St. Gregory with my cassock a bit disheveled, having been chased over a wall by a dog, and Mother gave the impression that it was a normal way to prepare for Mass. She would kiss the hands of the priest who had given her

Communion in thanks for having brought Jesus, but she had no illusions: More than once did I hear her say how people wherever she went felt betrayed by priests. Nonetheless she asked them to remember her as the drop of water mingled with the wine in the preparation of the chalice.

She silenced even a Jesuit who joked that she seemed to be getting smaller: "Yes, and I must get smaller until I am small enough to fit into the heart of Jesus." I still have the radiant memory of listening to her talk with my own mother on a visit to New York some years later, and it was like listening to two neighbors chatting over the backyard fence. Just as picturesque was the time in Rome when she led me by the hand through a large field of poppies on the periphery of the city and then served tea on a rickety table in the garden. Afterward, because there was a public transportation strike, she and another sister and I tried hitchhiking. No one gave us a lift, but Mother barely shrugged her shoulders.

I have a picture of her wearing an insulated coat such as meatpackers wear when she arrived in the Bronx one winter night. When that picture was taken she winced because of the cataracts that had swollen her eyes: "Jesus told me to let the people take pictures, so I told him to please let a soul out of Purgatory each time the light flashes." Her eyes could look ineffably sad, as when she heard that during Holy Hour in our hospice, a patient had hanged himself upstairs. There was no humbug about her. She could give orders like a Marine sergeant, and her counsel was pointed but not piercing. When she told me to correct a reporter who had misquoted her, I said, "I'll pray about it and then write." "No," she insisted, "we need this right away. I pray. You write."

After I had preached one morning, she pushed a book across the kitchen table: "Reading is good, but make your meditation before you preach and then just tell the people what Jesus told you." I had the sense that she was on a special wavelength. On my way to say Mass for her in New York, I found myself in the subway standing in front of a kiosk featuring magazines with women who were only innocent of the Legion of Decency. After Mass, although I had said nothing, she said, "On your way through the streets when you are coming to say Mass, don't look at the magazines with the women on the covers." By showing the utter naturalness of supernaturalness, saints are a sacrament of the transfiguration. All through the Christian annals it has seemed perfectly natural and not silly to tell them, "You gotta save Christianity. You gotta."

Philip Thomas Bayard Clayton

❧

To call Tubby Clayton Philip would be like calling Babe Ruth George. He was born in Queensland in 1885, and his parents returned to their native England when he was two. "I decided to accompany them," he wrote. He was just ten years younger than Chesterton, whom he knew as an old boy of St. Paul's School in London. Not even Chesterton's prototypical Father John O'Connor was more like Father Brown than Tubby, in every way except for his membership in the Henrician spin-off of Holy Church. In all other things—clothing askew, distracted look, Dickensian oratory—he was not eccentric but rather centric in a world gone tortuously eccentric in the Great War. I knew him as a Winant Volunteer, a group formed by Tubby for American college students to help rebuild blitzed-out London, even as late as the exhausted London of 1960s Carnaby Street.

After a first-class degree in theology from Oxford he was a curate in Portsea, but his star flamed when he became an army chaplain in 1915, opening Talbot House in Poperinghe. This hospice in Flanders survived until the German army invaded, a kind of club and relief center to thousands of soldiers gasping for normalcy in the horrible fields. As most of the officers were gentry, the sign read, "All rank abandon, ye who enter here." Talbot House remains as a museum, and the Belgian government put Tubby's picture on a postage stamp. Our own Father Brown formed the Toc H Movement (Toc being the army signaler's code for T), a worldwide organization of clubs dedicated to promoting the kind of fellowship and volunteer services that animated the Talbot House fraternity.

A trip to West Africa in 1932 inspired the British Empire Leprosy Relief Association, but Tubby's longest association was with All Hallows Church at the Tower of London where he was vicar and which he rebuilt after it was bombed in 1940. There he censured me for indulging the fad of brass rubbing: I guarded those rubbings with my life and now the Americans are rubbing them away. Dr. Johnson could not have surpassed his elegies on London. He solemnly informed me that only three peers in the House of Lords could trace their families back as far as any Cockney within the sound of All Hallows bells.

As a Companion of Honour and royal chaplain with a royal corgi from Her Royal Self, he prized as his greatest royal achievement public swimming baths along the Thames for poor children. When the London City Council employed all its Labourite bureaucracy to stymie his plans, he went to Buckingham Palace in red cloak, gaiters, buckled shoes, and tricorner hat; pocketed his ubiquitous pipe; stormed past the guard; and was ushered into the presence of King George VI. "Where do you want this bathing pool, Tubby?" "At the Tower, Your Majesty." "The Tower of London? I think I own that." "Indeed, Sir." One call on the imperial telephone fixed everything.

Some seven years before his death in 1972, I was with
him for a reunion in Belgium. Daily we walked through military cemeteries, and he stopped every so often to mutter to
a tombstone. In Tubby Clayton was man alive as man had
lived in the halcyon Edwardian afternoon of the world, and
in him too was the shudder of a world blasted apart, never
to be put together again. The last lines I shall forget, if a
time of forgetting comes, are those of Laurence Binyon that
we recited on acre after acre of grass and granite graves:

> They shall grow not old, as we that are left grow old:
> Age shall not weary them, nor the
>   years condemn.
> At the going down of the sun and
>   in the morning
> We will remember them.

Vernon A. Walters

❦

In the late sixteenth century Sir Henry Wotton said that an ambassador is an honest man sent to lie abroad for the good of his country. Benjamin Franklin modified that: A soldier dies for his country, while a diplomat lies for it. Vernon A. Walters was a soldier often in the line of fire and an ambassador incorrigibly honest. An aide to seven presidents, he helped shape the Marshall Plan, served as deputy director of the CIA, member of the NATO Standing Group, and ambassador to the United Nations and Germany. A behind-the-scenes man, he helped secure the release of American hostages in Lebanon while holding his UN post.

He had studied in Britain and France as the son of an immigrant British insurance salesman, but when his father suffered financial reverses, he returned to the United States, dropped out of school, and worked as an insurance claims investigator. The future lieutenant general was summoned as an army private to translate for a visiting Brazilian officer because he knew Spanish. When Walters informed his commanding officer that Brazilians speak Portuguese, he was ordered to learn it, which he seems to have done overnight. That was the start of his career as a translator in French, Portuguese, Spanish, Italian, German, Dutch, Russian, and respectable Chinese, all without a high school diploma. Years later, de Gaulle would say, "Nixon, you gave a magnificent speech, but your interpreter was eloquent." He accompanied the Nixons to Latin America, and when his mouth was cut as stones smashed their limousine in Caracas, the vice president told him, "Spit that glass out, you are going to have a lot more talking to do in Spanish for me today."

As an aide to General Mark Clark he entered Rome in triumph in 1944, giving a ride on his tank to the future King Hassan II of Morocco. He filmed Truman's meeting with MacArthur on Wake Island and took the only recorded notes when Truman fired the general. His silent missions included one visit to Castro and smuggling Henry Kissinger into Paris for the Vietnam peace talks. Kissinger stayed incognito in his apartment in Neuilly, and Walters once got him into France from Frankfurt under the pretext that he was the mistress of Georges Pompidou. When I recently asked Kissinger to summarize Walter's diplomacy, he instantly replied, "Flamboyant discretion." Dick Walters loved the drama of it all. As a teetotaling, nonsmoking, chaste bachelor, he was a kind of ascetic James Bond, with the added advantage that he was real.

He was the only one present during Eisenhower's negotiations at Rambouillet with de Gaulle. He was dashing enough to accompany Maurice Chevalier as an escort for ladies to the opera, and to him Clare Boothe Luce, upon being decorated with an Asiatic nation's Order of Chastity, Second Class, confided that she did not know if it was an honor or an insult.

In foreign negotiations, he stuck to his Catholic guns on eugenics issues and was a fervent promoter of orthodox Catholic institutions. Pastorally, I was aware of his regularity at the sacraments in Manhattan where he welcomed people on the front steps of church and took up the collection. A year before his death, I flew with him from Paris to New York, and even then, with flamboyant discretion, he mentioned mysteriously that he had been doing work for some North Africans. He colorfully described explaining Star Wars to Pope John Paul II, laden with maps. Our last time together was at a dinner where Helmut Kohl, his wife overwhelmed by a bizarre illness and only a few months short of suicide, embraced Dick, then in a wheelchair, and enjoyed the ambassador's mellifluous German. With bravery and integrity, Vernon Walters conjured a brand of diplomacy that fooled many who thought honesty was a clever deceit.

Orietta Doria-Pamphilj

❧

From the time I began studies in Rome in 1979, a matronly lady unknown to me often attended Mass in our college chapel near the Trevi Fountain. She would arrive gingerly in a housedress on a bicycle, with loaves of bread in the basket. One day after preaching I was invited to tea at her house down the street. I thought I had the wrong address. Her palazzo had 900 rooms, five courtyards, five monumental staircases, and a Baroque chapel whose foundations tradition claimed had been the prison of St. Paul. In 1992 she donated to the Church the family church designed by Borromini, St. Agnes on the Piazza Navona. There was also a Norman castle in Apulia, a thirteenth-century abbey near Portofino, and land in Genoa. Admiral Andrea Doria was a champion of Lepanto, and more luster was added by Pope Innocent X. My bicycle lady was the Princess Doria-Pamphilj, four times a princess, twice a duchess, and eight times a marchesa. The family inherited much in 1790 when Clement XIII resolved the claims of the Borghese, Colonnas, and Dorias by settling on Prince Giovanni Doria the name and estates of Girolamo Pamphilj, who died without male issue.

The only time I heard anything like self-regard from her was one afternoon when she recounted the state visit of George V during which Queen Mary had called on her mother. But even that was in a conversation about complicated alliances: Her great-grandfather had married Lady Mary Talbot, whom he had met at the coronation of Queen Victoria, and she was related to the Earls of Shrewsbury and Dukes of Newcastle. In 1958, after the death of her father, who had withheld consent, she married a British naval officer, Frank Pogson, valiant in the war and less successful in introducing cricket to Italy in the family park, the Villa Doria-Pamphilj, larger than the Vatican. Her father, Prince Filippo Andrea IV, was a leader of the anti-Fascist resistance, plotting in his own palace as Mussolini harangued the crowds across the Piazza San Marco, the shouting echoing in the sixteenth-century corridors of the palace where Handel and Corelli had made music. The prince was released from prison only to be persecuted by the Nazis for protecting the Jews of Rome. The young Princess Orietta and her mother hid for a while with their laundress, taking in washing, disguised by soaking their smooth hands in lye.

The family's art collection really took off when Camillo Pamphilj, nephew of Innocent V, married the widow of Paolo Borghese in 1647. Princess Orietta's favorite small drawing room was at the end of endless halls (there were a ballroom, several untouched eighteenth-century drawing rooms, and one dining room done in the dark paneling of a Bavarian hunting lodge, where during our happy meals Frank liked to pursue his progressive views on Catholic matters, all the while recommending Santa Maria in Cosmedin for its freedom from modern liturgical depredations). One passed Raphael, Titian, Caravaggio, Tintoretto, and Bernini's bust and Velazquez's portrait of Pope Innocent, but I remember only one decoration in her little parlor: unframed crayon drawings by her two adopted children.

Frank died in 1998 and his wife two years later, a month after Queen Elizabeth II visited in the footsteps of her grandmother. An old cardinal told a seminarian that it would take a year to learn all about Rome and a lifetime to know nothing about it. *"Roma, non basta una vita."* If a lifetime is not enough, Orietta had many lifetimes in her as she bicycled to Mass. She claimed to know every pothole in those streets. As Charles I prayed that he might go from one crown to another, so it is noble to think that my old neighbors of ghostly grandeur have gone to grander halls.

Hugh Maycock

❧

As a summer student in 1967, I banged the heavy knocker on the old door of the Gothic Revival building on St. Giles Street in Oxford. Consuelo Vanderbilt had been a neighbor after her divorce from the duke of Marlborough. St. Edmund Campion walked those acres often when he was at St. John's College. My model theologian, Austin Farrer, frequently came by, and there was a nameless man with a pince-nez who used a large ear trumpet to hear High Mass.

The Rev. Hugh Maycock (1903–1980) who greeted me was rarely hailed by his first name in the Californian manner, although he was Uncle Hugh in his absence. As principal of Pusey House, he oversaw a library and residence hall thrust up as a blatant celebration of the Tractarian movement. It was aware of being more Catholic liturgically than the Catholics, and the chapel, designed by Temple Moore and Ninian Comper, where generations including John Betjeman and Harold Macmillan served at the altar, still glows in Edwardian gilt. After my first stay I occasionally returned and, years later, I became a member of St. Cross College, which has taken over some of the property.

Besides preserving the death mask of Dr. Pusey in his
carbuncular glory, the house has an 80,000-volume library,
mainly history and patristics. *Deus scientiarum Dominus* was
the motto, and I passed golden days just for reading and
occasional punting down the river. One long croquet
match provoked complaint from the rarely uncomposed
Uncle Hugh about the incessant din of mallets. He never
objected when I practiced Elgar on the chapel organ,
which, inexplicably, had come from Brattleboro, Vermont.
His own hobby was collecting antique pawnbroker's balls
whose history he traced to the Medici.

Inordinate sleep was a necessity for him after he was
bitten by the tsetse fly in Malawi as a missionary. "I can
always tell what time of day it is. When I awake in my
pajamas I know it is time for Mass and when I awake in my
trousers I know it is time for tea." Being a clergyman of the
Church of England in its mellow sunset years, he pacifi-
cally regarded what it had been, with no delusions about
what was happening to it. Abroad was worse: In liturgical
processions, American bishops waddle. He spoke seldom
at table. Occasionally some singular humor broke forth:
"I say, if your name were Baden Baden I could ask, 'Have
you ever been to Baden Baden, Baden Baden?'" Notice of
his amiable little ways began upon his arrival in 1955 from
Cambridge, where he was vicar of Little St. Mary's and
had published a tract on original sin: a comforting doctrine
because, since Adam did it, it's not our fault. He imputed
eccentricity to another only once in my presence. A maths
don in his undergraduate days had developed a conceit that
he was turning into a mushroom, like Gaius Caligula who

thought he was made of glass. Uncle Hugh added, rather chillingly I thought, that there was no truth to it.

Wearing a World War I style flying helmet, he drove me to a pub in ancient Newbridge, steering along the right side of the road in tribute to my American citizenship. We survived, but his successor as principal did not. The Australian fell off a ladder shortly after his arrival and died within hours. Uncle Hugh told the press that the incident had caused confusion, and confusion he most disdained. His next successor, Cheslyn Jones, was a Welsh narcoleptic, often falling asleep in mid-sentence. Rooms that had heard the voices of Charles Gore, Darwell Stone, F. L. Cross, Evelyn Waugh, Dorothy Sayers, C. S. Lewis, and Tolkien never knew anything like that awkward silence. I suppose it was the last slumber of a way of life vanished now like the Cheshire Cat, but enchanting when it was.

John Paul II

❧

I began my seminary studies by flying to Rome the same day Pope John Paul II returned from his first apostolic visit to the United States. Some published reports implied that I had been piled into his craft, but I was on the flight behind his, and I definitely had not been kidnapped.

The early years of his pontificate were an unending round of surprises. Visiting both Britain and Argentina during the Falklands War ranked high among them, and to a reporter who asked how he could do this for belligerents, his response raised the eyebrows of some soft ecclesiologists: "This is my Church." He had a definite sense of that. Although Queen Elizabeth II had been told she need not follow the protocol that reserved white for Catholic queens, her arrival in audience veiled in black with multiple diamonds moved him to a palpable kind of childlike delight; after all, she had been on currency and stamps around the world when he was unknown. He did not lose balance, though, and later that day he unofficially chuckled kindly in recounting that she had told him they both had the burden of heading a Church.

In pontifical ceremonies, nascent seminarians and newly oiled deacons often stood closer to him than important officials. Once in St. Peter's a screaming madwoman in a flaming red dress dashed in front of me toward the altar. Guards quickly knocked her legs out from under her and gracefully carried her away in what almost seemed like a ballet. The pope never blinked. He did wince on a Palm Sunday when he blessed a rose-crowned lamb presented at the offertory. I was near enough, as a deacon, to see his face contort as he touched the lamb's head. Weeks later, in the same place, he was shot, and I refuse to call hindsight what seemed to be a presentiment. On May 13, a woman came to our college residence on Via dell'Umilta to collect her audience ticket and, after she was shot in the attack on the Holy Father, I think it was her blood one saw on the stones. All that night an icon of Our Lady of Czestochowa rested on the empty papal throne.

He met my visiting parents, who were not yet Catholic, and instead of discussing the papal primacy he took their hands and mine and made a kind of sandwich of them between his own. Within little more than a year they were received into the Church. The only personal contribution I made to his pontificate was at a frugal Lenten dinner when he asked the English word for homiletics and I told him, homiletics.

Laws of logic check breezy attempts to install him in a diaphanous pantheon of the valiant while rejecting his claims for the papacy. A man who mistakenly thinks of himself as the Rock on which the Church was founded is great in the sense of being greatly deluded and roams

history as a cultural vandal. If he is right, he deserves
religious obedience.

I did not appreciate his poetry or drama, and supposed
that what sounded turgid was lost in translation, as is the
almost inevitable way with verse. It was tempting to neglect
some of his paradoxes as romantic flights, too. That was
my instinct when he told our race, "Man, become what
you are." In the reflected light of those Roman years, those
of us who heard him were like the men on the Emmaus
road wondering why he did not notice the sunset when all
the while he was squinting at a sunrise. In various ways,
shouting over Marxist goons in Nicaragua, patiently abiding the harangues of an American bourgeois, he was saying, "O foolish and slow of heart, not to believe all that
the prophets said must come to pass." After his Amen as
he left this act of his life, we may say: "Did not our hearts
burn within us when he walked with us and opened to us
the Scriptures along the way?"

Terence Cardinal Cooke

❦

"Oh, just one more thing." After an hour of incidental conversation on September 6, 1981, Terence Cardinal Cooke (1921–1983) mentioned as an aside that at my ordination two days later it might be good to have a few guards to prevent any difficulties. Hierarchs of the Episcopal Church objected to my ordination, since they had previously ordained me. As it was the judgment of the Catholic Church that Henry VIII was not a prophet and I was not a valid priest, I was to be ordained unconditionally. Terence Cooke would have rather died than contradict doctrine and, at the ceremony in the Lady Chapel of St. Patrick's Cathedral, he read a statement urging good will all around. He also repulsed the requests of the rector of the cathedral, who had Anglican friends, that I be ordained inconspicuously in the cardinal's private chapel and that no hymn of John Henry Newman be sung. Master of the velvet glove, Cardinal Cooke smilingly ordered that we sing "Lead, Kindly Light."

His mother, a native of County Galway like his father, died when he was nine. The world to him was parochial, and he moved from parish school in the Bronx to minor seminary and then to major seminary and studied social work at the Catholic University of America. He was never a parish pastor. In serving writs he made such a name that he soon became an articled clerk: Francis Cardinal Spellman sought no prodigy but he did want an efficient administrator such as Cardinal Cooke as seminary procurator. From the cardinal's secretary in 1957, he became vice chancellor in 1958, chancellor in 1961, and vicar general and auxiliary bishop in 1965.

Martin Luther King Jr. was shot on the day of Cooke's installation, and the new archbishop went to Harlem. There was still a legacy of prelacy to bank on, and he was received with respect, but the photographs of his return from Rome as cardinal are poignant, when his motorcade was hailed with red roses. The aura was stale, and no prelate would be received that way again. An inter-parish finance commission propped up poor parishes, but he opened only four new parishes after Spellman had opened forty-five, and the archdiocesan elementary school enrollment dropped by one-half. His devotion to detail left large financial reserves that would quickly disperse after he died.

His death on October 6, 1983, focused a nation. After eight years contending with lymphoma, he was gathered up as a patriarch, writing letters to the flock. It was a tonic to the faithful after the archbishop of Chicago had died amid rancor. Even the urbane, who thought Cardinal Cooke soporific, admired such a finale.

We dined often during his visits to Rome, and his beribboned documents once stopped a lecture by Ugo Cardinal Poletti in the *aula magna* of the Lateran University to expedite my diaconal ordination. In 1983, I received a surprise telephone call from him telling me that my parents were Catholic. He had received them in their village in Westchester County without fuss before lunch, the last souls he would bring into the Church before he took to his deathbed. "We really pulled one over on George," he told them.

Only once did I watch his anger flare, at the mention of a degenerate liturgist. His aversion to confrontation was droll. Had he, in place of Pope Leo, met Attila at the gates of Rome, he might have changed the subject to the weather. Yet there is the case of St. Januarius's blood liquefying in Cardinal Cooke's presence out of season. Only the Church can determine the difference between prosaic convention and heroic temperance. He told a radical cleric who insulted him in the garish 1970s: "I may not be the smartest man, but I have a good memory." In matters pertaining to holy Truth, his memory was more than half as old as time.

Helen Taft Manning

❧

Her books on *The Revolt of French Canada* and *British Colonial Government After the American Revolution* remain standard references, but Helen Taft Manning (1891–1987) was far more interesting talking history in the 1970s when I knew her in Pennsylvania. She had become dean of Bryn Mawr College at the age of twenty-five, was acting president twice, and was professor of history from 1930 to her retirement in 1956. As the wife of a history professor at Yale, where she had taken her doctorate, and the mother of two daughters, she contradicted a maxim of the astringently unnatural M. Carey Thomas who, as a founding mother of Bryn Mawr, opined that only the college's failures married. A sophomoric Katherine Hepburn was nearly expelled by her for low grades. From early years she was a suffragette, while not sharing Dr. Thomas's impatience of convention on the subject.

A few weeks after she was born, Edison patented his motion picture camera, of which she would approve, while sensibly frowning on lesser inventions like mixed drinks and aerated bread. By paternal inheritance she was a Unitarian but was formed by Episcopalianism in the maternal line and widely embraced more traditional religious views. She told me that the first African cardinal, Laurean Rugambwa, exclaimed that she was the only one he had ever met who had known Pope Leo XIII. Her brother Charles, a mayor of her native Cincinnati, helped found the World Council of Churches and was the youngest president of the International YMCA. Their father was president of another institution known as the United States of America.

A photo of the family in Manila, absent brother Robert (the future senator), included their governess, who taught her German and a little Tagalog. It was in the interest of fixing a fair price for church lands that her father, as governor of the Philippines, had met with the pope and had taken her along when she was ten years old. She confided in an unpublished sentiment that her father thought the Chinese and the Spanish noble races but that a tempest brewed when they commingled. My impression was that the bad blood between Taft and Roosevelt began with dislike for Teddy's bumptious ways by her mother, whose ardent campaigning he thought unwomanly. After the First Lady's stroke, teenaged Helen served as White House hostess, assisting her father in serving full suppers rather than the frail buffets customarily offered at the end of receiving lines. Although her father was not unyielding to the temptations of the groaning board, she wanted it known that his 350-pound frame was the mountainous resolution of a glandular injury he had suffered in a childhood fall from a carriage.

Taft was the lovely kind of kindly man whose bewilderment by unkindness rendered him incapable of intelligent response. As progressivist pressure against his administration increased, he took solace in automobile drives on which his daughter often accompanied him. The bellowing of Bull Moose demagogues ensured Taft's defeat, but it was his wife and not he who had wanted the White House. His prize came when Harding appointed him chief justice; and when the family went to Buckingham Palace in 1922, the former president wore his judicial robes for their official portrait with George and Mary.

On March 8, 1930, Herbert Hoover was taking a quiet motor drive in the established tradition and only heard of Taft's death when he returned to the White House. He was received at the Taft house on Wyoming Avenue by the two Helens, neither of whose faces launched a thousand ships, but one who gave Washington its cherry trees and the younger one who lived to see the misery of telephones in automobiles.

Chauncey Devereux Stillman

꙳

Of wealth and war Chauncey Devereux Stillman (1907–1989) knew much and said little. He did write a life of his great-grandfather Charles who left colonial roots in Connecticut to establish a fortune in Mexican cotton, real estate, and silver mines. Moving north to Texas, he helped bankroll an attempted invasion of Mexico by Carbajal and founded Brownsville, much of which he bequeathed to his son James who became president of what is now the Citigroup bank. By the end of the Civil War, Charles Stillman was one of the richest men in America. John D. Rockefeller's brother William had two daughters who married two of James's sons. One of the couples bore a son named for Chauncey Depew, head of the New York Central Railroad.

In his country home in Dutchess County, now a museum he endowed, is a youthful portrait that makes it easy to imagine Chauncey in Paris in the Roaring Twenties. In 1942, the future commodore of the New York Yacht Club donated his gorgeous flagship *Westerly* as a patrol boat on the lookout for German submarines. As squadron air combat intelligence officer on the USS *Enterprise*, he fought in the Battle of Leyte Gulf in October of 1944 and wrote the history of his Air Group 20, which in three months sank thirty-three ships and destroyed 345 enemy airplanes. Later he served as a staff officer with the National Security Council.

Schools and charities flourished by his philanthropy, especially after his embrace of Catholicism. The Gentleman of His Holiness was an efficient cause of many of the Church's most vigorous new academic and cultural institutions. One regret Chauncey vouchsafed to me in this regard was the abuse of the chair of Roman Catholic Studies that he had endowed at the Harvard Divinity School. Christopher Dawson was its first holder until 1962, and Stillman thereby was the chief publicist of that formerly neglected genius, but since then the professorship has gone the unhappy way of the school itself. The university ignored Chauncey as curtly as it had eagerly accepted his largesse. The day after our discussion, the incumbent professor unexpectedly died.

His 1,200-acre Wethersfield estate declared a lifelong enthusiasm for nature and wildlife preservation. Ten acres of formal Italian gardens were designed by Evelyn Poehler, whose husband Fred was one of the last great beaux arts architects. Chauncey promoted the current revival of classical design and, with his own degree in architecture from Columbia University, built his Georgian house with its collection of Toulouse-Lautrec, Sargent, Degas, and numerous Cassatts. (Mary's family had the Pennsylvania Railroad and were old friends of the Stillmans.) A Murillo hung in his chapel. Pietro Annigoni spent a year painting frescoes in the Gloriette, a ballroom that was a frisky variant of the

Sistine Chapel. He would surrender his own bedroom so that I could wake up facing Gilbert Stuart's Washington. The prize of all was *The Halberdier* by Pontormo. Had Stillman not decided at the last minute to risk flying it over from Italy for an early exhibition, it would have gone down with the Andrea Doria. Sale of it in 1989 for $34 million, then the highest price ever paid for an Old Master, helped to fund a foundation for Catholic culture.

Aesthetics did not throttle ascetics, and when he was dying of lung cancer I occasionally met him praying the Rosary in a hideously modern Manhattan basement chapel. The last Mass he heard was in his Madison Avenue apartment, and his whispered request of me was that the sign of peace be omitted "because the butler finds it awkward." I obliged the Gentleman of His Holiness and the gentleman's gentleman, and I perpetuate that final wish as often as I can.

Richard Eberhart

✿

O dd it seems to see a historical marker on the house of Richard Eberhart (1904–2005). My English class met there weekly in the early 1960s before the pillars of our firmament were pulled down by the cultural chaos of ugly years panting to break forth. As Poet-in-Residence at Dartmouth, having been Poet Laureate at the Library of Congress for a couple of years, he taught us to write in front of the fireplace at 5 Webster Terrace, a short walk to Occom Pond. In winter we played ice hockey on that pond, for indoor hockey seemed a contradiction in terms. Mrs. Eberhart, Betty, was hospitable, and her family's company, Butcher's Wax in Boston, helped to polish the poet's income.

That the relentlessly benign, pipe-smoking, elfin endomorph would live a full 101 years was never a conjecture to sophomores who thought all professors were beyond chronological reference. He was barely sixty when he used a poem of mine to inaugurate a new printing press using antique typeset. To 5 Webster Terrace came a parade of poets better known to the world than to undergraduates (for all learning is post-graduate), and we refreshed them with our blithe insouciance. "Mr. Warren, do your friends call you Robert or Penn?" "Mr. Tate, have you been writing very long?" Alan Tate was the first Catholic metaphysical poet to enter my universe.

Eberhart had a reserved religious sense and was a fixture in the local Episcopal church. Some said he was a relic of Henri Bergson, whose convert to Catholicism informed the professor's governing maxims: "Poems in a way are spells against death," and "Style is the perfection of a point of virtue." He had been Robert Lowell's teacher at St. Mark's School but only obliquely referred to Lowell's pirouette with Catholicism. He did speak of Lowell as of a son, albeit a manic one. He was paternal with us, too, writing chatty notes to our parents. The friend of Eliot and the Sitwells, in all his sophistication he could not bring himself to tell us the content of Oscar Wilde's crime. In this I think we were not ignorant but rather innocent, in a way incomprehensible now to an earthly city invaded by the Vulgar tribe.

Eberhart's piercing eye for the death of things began with his mother's death when he was a teenager, just before his father lost his fortune: "In June, amid the golden fields / I saw a groundhog lying dead. / Dead lay he; my senses shook / and mind outshot our naked frailty." He continued on to Cambridge University after graduating from Dartmouth and worked on a tramp steamer. A favorite story was of spending 1931 and 1932 as tutor to the son of the king of Siam. When King Prajadhipok, with 600 pieces of luggage, came to New York for eye surgery, Eberhart took the royal entourage to the Cotton Club in Harlem. After surgery, all bowed as the king's cataract was carried around on a silken pillow. Experience of World War II

service in the navy produced "The Fury of Aerial Bom-
bardment." In the first stanza, "the infinite spaces" are still
silent paraphrases of Pascal in the *Pensées*: "*Le silence eternel de
ces espaces infinis meffraye.*" Latterly the Bollingen Prize and all
the usual decorations came to him. I may claim a Pulitzer
Prize-winning semicolon, for he asked me to help edit his
anthology that got the award in 1966, and the semicolon
was the one suggestion of mine that he took.

As the last of the post-World War I academic poets,
flashing sestinas and villanelles, he read Ginsberg to us,
with the unction of an anthropologist unveiling a howl-
ing curiosity. Professor Eberhart took another tack, and in
a pleasant house now marked with a tablet as though the
house itself had died, he read to teenaged scriveners of a
"Mystery made visible / This lyric mortal loveliness / The
earth breathing, and the sun."

Hildegarde Sell

❦

A woman who sang on television in 1937 can be said to have had a long career. A priest at St. John's Cathedral High School in Milwaukee had told Hildegarde Sell (1906–2005) to give up thoughts of the convent and, when lack of funds thwarted the Marquette University student's classical music studies, she played the piano in silent film theaters and then barged into vaudeville. After some lean years plugging songs for Irving Berlin, she found fame in Europe with an inflated report of King Gustav's infatuation with her. Overcoming a slight German accent bred from her family, owners of a Bavarian delicatessen in New Holstein, Wisconsin, she soon was able to sing in the language of any army that happened to be invading whatever country she was touring. Her manager, Anna Sosenko, wrote her Franglaise signature song, "Darling, Je Vous Aime Beaucoup," and for the rest of her life she was doused in blue stage lights, tossing red roses from her opera-gloved hands. Much later this image would inspire the Muppet Miss Piggy, and performers like Liberace copied her style of using just one name. George and Ira Gershwin hymned her in "My Cousin from Milwaukee," and Walter Winchell dubbed her "the Incomparable Hildegarde." She was called the First Lady of the Supper Clubs by Eleanor Roosevelt.

At the Waldorf, the Duchess of Windsor thought Hildegarde was too familiar with the Duke, but she traveled with her own orchestra, earning startling salaries and astonishing women in the 1940s with an annual budget of $10,000 for clothes. *Ad Majorem Dei Gloriam*, the best silk evening gowns were tailored into chasubles for missionary priests. Hildegarde was an evangelist, too, in her own circle: The novelist Jacqueline Susann was not the only convert she sponsored in baptism. A century-long lifespan vindicates her book of health and cosmetic advice, *Over 50, So What!*, which can seem theologically diaphanous: "I pray to St. Jude while having my skin treatment that he'll make the preparation work." In Manhattan at the Church of St. Agnes, where she was a daily communicant, she once interrupted my thanksgiving prayers after Mass to ask of me: "What kind of facial soap do you use?" When I replied that I had not the slightest idea, she could not have looked more surprised if I had told her I was an Albigensian.

It was her devout but ill-advised custom to sing "The Old Rugged Cross" on Good Friday. When it devolved upon me to preach the Three Hours, I stopped that as delicately as I could. On a previous Good Friday, she had poured her heart into that song as Archbishop Fulton Sheen preached and Clare Boothe Luce read the Lamentations of Jeremiah. At 3 p.m., the archbishop announced the death of Christ and then joined hands with Hildegarde and Mrs. Luce for a full stage bow to applause. That vignette, along with others like Hildegarde touring hospital wards on the arm of the preening Dr. Tom Dooley, was a warning that something was not altogether well in Zion. The neuralgic confusion of glitter and grace was too out of synch with the true drama of man to dismiss it as mere kitsch, but neither was it humbug, for it was not cynical.

Our Hildegarde was a third-order Carmelite and was praying the Rosary in the Carmelite nursing home when I last visited her. The only image on the wall was the Sacred Heart in the old kind of bad Sulpician style that moved people to pray before some churches became plush cabarets in the 1950s. The Incomparable Hildegarde was named for the Blessed Hildegarde of Bingen, a singer who wrote reams of health and beauty advice. Hildegarde said cryptically that, unlike the saint of Bingen, "I won't die wondering." I think she meant it as an act of faith.

Ignatius Cardinal Kung Pin-Mei

❧

s my Cantonese is not what it would have been had I
been present at Pentecost, in 1999 I led the interces-
sory prayers in French and Latin at a Solemn Mass on
the seventieth priestly ordination anniversary, fiftieth episcopal anniversary, twentieth cardinalatial anniversary, and
ninety-eighth birth anniversary of Ignatius Kung (Gong)
Pin-Mei in his home of exile in Stamford, Connecticut.
Never fear: St. Peter was very alive in the serene cardinal
who had been bound in his old age and taken where he
would not.

Born in 1901, his family had been Catholic for at least
five generations. An aunt, who was a nun, tutored him in
Chinese classics and religion as preparation for a Jesuit high
school founded by French missionaries. After ordination
as a diocesan priest at the age of twenty-nine, he taught
in Jesuit schools; when Shanghai was seized by the Communists in 1949, he was consecrated bishop of Soochow,
becoming bishop of Shanghai and apostolic administrator
of Soochow and Nanking the following year. His family
sensed that it was a prison sentence, although a photograph of the slight, young bishop shows no foreboding.

He rallied the Legion of Mary to a holy militancy, and soon many were sentenced to decades of hard labor. Their message to him was Petrine: "Bishop, in darkness, you light up our path. You guide us on our treacherous journey. You uphold our faith and the traditions of the Church. You are the foundation rock of our Church in Shanghai."

In 1953 he gathered 3,000 young men in the cathedral while a thousand women recited the Rosary in the square. As police surrounded them, they processed with a large cross chanting: "Long live the Bishop. Long live the Holy Father. Long live the Church." In 1955 the bishop was thrust before a microphone at a show trial in a stadium to recant his anti-social errors, but he shouted: "Long live Christ the King! Long live the Pope!" The sentence was life imprisonment. When frequently urged to denounce the pope, he ritually answered: "I am a Roman Catholic bishop. If I denounce the Holy Father, not only would I not be a bishop, I would not even be a Catholic. You can cut off my head, but you can never take away my duties." For thirty years, much of it in solitary confinement, the Mass was forbidden, along with the Bible. His Communions were of the heart, all the time resisting the proselytizing of the collaborationist Chinese Catholic Patriotic Association. When international pressure got him released under house arrest, the government choreographed a propaganda dinner with the visiting Cardinal Sin of Manila, but the bishops were not allowed to speak to each other. The canny cardinal proposed that the sullen gathering be enlivened with songs. When his turn came, Kung chanted the *"Tu es Petrus."*—"Thou art Peter, and on this rock I will build my Church."

With stomach cancer at the age of eighty-six, he was sent to Hong Kong where he was amazed that Catholics no longer observed the Friday abstinence that he had kept for thirty meatless years. Eventually he settled in with his nephew Joseph in Connecticut, eager to return to the people of Shanghai as their bishop. Pope John Paul II told him that he had made him a cardinal secretly, *in pectore*, in 1979. They kept the secret until 1991, and on June 28 in St. Peter's Square, Kung rose from his wheelchair, threw away his cane, and walked up the steps to kneel before the pontiff and receive the red hat, as the crowd applauded for an unprecedented seven minutes.

The Kung family invited my mother to sit with them at the cardinal's funeral on March 18, 2000. It was the last Requiem she attended before her own death. All sang what Cardinal Kung taught millions: "There is one thing against which the gates of hell shall not prevail."

Wellington Mara

❦

The last time I saw Wellington Mara (1916–2005) dancing was at my birthday party. He and Ann, married more than fifty years, allowed that we had been good friends for more than twenty years because I held professional football in contempt and never asked them for tickets.

His father, Tim, a legal bookmaker who had never seen a football game, bought the rights to a football team in New York for $500, according to one story. In their first home game, the Giants lost to the Frankford Yellow Jackets. Wellington was fourteen when his father gave the team to him and his brother Jack. From the early days at the Polo Grounds, to which my father would take me as to a shrine because it was home to the baseball Giants, the football Giants went on to Yankee Stadium and eventually to the New Jersey Meadowlands, now regularly filling the 76,000-seat Giants Stadium.

Wellington became the chief architect of the National Football League. His men were not little men: Gifford, Rote, Robustelli, Brown, and Grier, with Landry and Lombardi among assistant coaches, and even the most raucous revered the dignity of Duke. Among his countless philanthropies nothing surpassed his ardor for right-to-life causes. His Life Athletes use their star power to instruct young boys at summer camps in chastity and respect for life. Wellington knew me well enough not to wince when on a boat ride I asked one of these, tight end Mark Bavaro, who he was.

If he danced at my party, he mourned at my mother's funeral, and he must have broken the record for attending baptisms and first communions, as the father of eleven children and grandfather of more than forty. He and Ann attended daily Mass all their lives and raised their children in the faith. When Christmas approached, his note on the refrigerator, where teenagers are wont to gather, read: "No Confession, No Santa." The rosary he was buried holding was not decoration: he prayed it constantly each day. At his death the expected bromides poured forth: "Wellington was in heaven looking down from God's skybox," and other formulaic pastiches of solid religion. But the long lines at his wake over two days and the overflowing cathedral and stopped traffic in midtown Manhattan were tributes to a grand man.

Rarely was his serenity ruffled. At the training camp soon after a dismal loss during the 1999 season, half of his players were gone. He did not conceal his contempt for Mario Cuomo's dissembling on abortion: The Church has never changed its teaching on the sanctity of human life; it didn't make up a rule for the convenience of a particular time like a rule at a country club, as the Governor would have us believe. When the team was doing poorly, a local sportswriter sneered in print: "What can you expect from an Irishman named Wellington, whose father was a bookmaker?" He replied at the next kickoff luncheon: "I'll tell you what you can expect. You can expect anything he says or writes may be repeated aloud in your own home in front of your own children. You can believe that he was taught to love and respect all mankind, but to fear no man. And you can believe that his abiding ambitions were to pass on to his family the true richness of the inheritance he received from his father, the bookmaker: the knowledge and love and fear of God, and second, to give you a Super Bowl winner."

I visited him in the hospital as he was dying from cancerous lymph nodes. He was not dancing, but he was smiling and trying to walk. He told his eldest son: "I'll be there when you get there." After he was taken home, a television was wheeled in so he might watch his team for a final time. Playing against Denver, the Giants won on a touchdown pass with five seconds left. The players shouted, "Duke! Duke! Duke!"

James Charles Risk

✣

I never saw James Charles Risk (1913–2005) in a plain
business suit. A dinner jacket without decorations was to
him tantamount to aboriginal nudity. Lifelong interest
in numismatics led to the study of royal orders and decorations, plenty of which garnished his wiry frame.

Like all civilized men who find time for high things in
dark times, he managed to publish *British Orders and Decorations*, a harbinger of his masterwork on *The Yale University
Brasher Doubloon*, while defying German attacks in the navy in
1943. For thirty-five years he worked for the Coin Gallery
in New York and discovered the King of Coins, an 1804
silver dollar proof coin that was the original in a set given by
President Andrew Jackson to the King of Siam in 1834.

In one photograph he smiles wryly at dinner with
me and my long-suffering German tutor, a vital Austrian baroness who fascinated him because of her direct
descent from a field marshal whose neglect of military
form in 1848 gained him the nickname the Butcher of
Hungary. In full flash of white tie, like a defiant light-
ning rod, Jim sports medals of the Orders of St. John in
Jerusalem, Sts. Maurice and Lazarus, the Crown of Italy,

Malta, St. George, and the badge of the Royal Victorian Order, of which he was the only living American member. A privilege of the last was to take tea once every three years with the Queen, for whom he catalogued her private collection of orders and decorations and who always called him *sui generis*.

After early years in Forest Hills, New York, and Upper Montclair, New Jersey, Jim graduated from Dartmouth in 1936 and following graduate studies at Harvard taught history at M.I.T. In 1940 he enlisted in the active naval reserve and was soon assigned to anti-submarine and convoy escort duty in the North Atlantic. He also participated in the invasion of Sicily. In an eccentric case of the navy not wasting a man's talents, he was ordered to write the administrative history of Mediterranean naval operations and then served the Allied Commission on the Democratization of Italy.

As protocol officer between the Vatican and the Quirinal Palace, he had frequent contacts with Pope Pius XII. Once he substituted for an unvarnished American general who cancelled a papal audience to play golf in Florence. For half an hour he and the pope chatted, neither letting on that he was not the general. On the night of the referendum on the monarchy, he watched Communists destroy ballots outside the Ministry of the Interior and deduced that the Americans allowed the interior minister, Togliatti, to fix the vote in favor of a republic. King Umberto and he visited every year thereafter in Cascais, Portugal. His gift for friendship embraced the Duke of Wellington, and he often stayed with him at Stratfield Saye and attended the Garter Service at Windsor in a front seat.

This lover of intrigue spent eleven days on the Trans-Siberian Express to take up a posting as vice consul in Vladivostok. As vice consul in Vietnam, which he always pronounced Indochine Française, he went on a hunting party with the Emperor Bao Dai, who held a sumptuous banquet in a tent in the jungle. At the end, the emperor stood up and relieved himself before all the ambassadors and their wives, very unlike the protocols of the Royal Victorian Order.

Jim threw off the Calvinism that had shackled his youth and became a Catholic during his sojourn in Rome. Blandishments of privilege vitiated the convert's zeal, and he reverted to ushering in a Protestant church; but in twilight time his chivalric ranks all rattled and he attended a Mass in my church, arranged by the Prince of Savoy. A year before he died, he was reconciled to the Holy Church and anointed, receiving Communion in his last months from a knight of Malta.

Bernard Basset

❧

quick Internet search for Rev. Bernard Basset (1909–1988) will provide a lot more information about St. Bernard, and the showing of hounds, than what pertains to this Jesuit who was one of the world's beguiling retreat directors.

Much of his appeal was from an enthusiasm for fugitive shards of joy: Recorded retreat addresses have repeated appeals to walk in the garden and take in the phlox and hibiscus. He did not conceal his lifelong talent as a pantomime librettist. For more than thirty years his transatlantic familiarity with America made him an ecclesiastical sort of P. G. Wodehouse. He was the rare clergyman of whom it is not pejorative to say that everyone liked him. Everyone I knew, anyway, except a former pastor of the Church of St. Agnes in Manhattan, and that may have been only momentary. Father Basset told me that the greatest failure of his life was preaching the Three Hours on Good Friday there and ending too soon. Monsignor Brew was furious that this Englishman had shortened our Lord's Passion and let him know it.

If in him there seemed no darkness at all, some who lived in perpetual storm clouds considered that eccentric.

John Stuart Mill thought that a paucity of eccentricity was dangerous: The amount of eccentricity in a society has generally been proportional to the amount of genius, mental vigor, and moral courage it contained. Father Bernard gloried in that triad. From an old Catholic family, going back to recusant times, he was sent to Stonyhurst. A fellow schoolboy there, Tom Burns, remembered a tall, stooping, bespectacled figure, a non-stop talker with a high voice and somewhat haughty intonation. His was an old-fashioned, family-formed sort of piety. It came to be increasingly seasoned with a light-hearted cynicism and irrepressible sense of fun, all of which developed into genuine spirituality.

For more than twenty years he wrote very funny Christmas essays for *The Tablet*, and the humor threaded his long line of books, the first of which was *We Neurotics*. His heyday was in the 1960s and 1970s, publishing such titles as *Priest in the Presbytery: A Psycho-ecclesiastical Extravaganza*. An English provincial called his history of the English Jesuits from Campion to Martindale a magnificent tale racily told. While distrusting the tendency to call any new book a classic if you agree with it entirely, I expect his chronicles of the Jesuits to be around at least as long as his biography of Thomas More, *Born for Friendship*, which raises the chancellor up and sits him with a tankard of ale across your kitchen table. If we wish to pray well, he wrote, then reading is vital, any reading that helps us to pay attention and to maintain our search for God. His prayer bore evangelical fruit. He reinvigorated the Sodalities of Our Lady in England, and his confessional became a school of prayer.

The Society of Jesus made room for his singular personality, as it had done in another sphere for Gerard Manley

Hopkins. After eight years as a parish priest in the Scilly Isles, he moved near Newman's old haunts in Littlemore. There he lived in the long shadows of the Oxford spires where in bright youth he had finished a brilliant degree. Overlong illness encumbered his twilight but was no burden to his ebullience while in the Catholic nursing home on Oxfords Cowley Road. Both legs had been amputated, and he related this with sparkling and unaffected cheerfulness. Several months after the first leg, the doctors advised removing the second, and this relieved him of the fuss of being fitted for an artificial limb. I saw him days before he died and his parting words were: "I have loved St. Ignatius and Newman. All my life I have studied them. But had I to do it over again, I'd have read nothing but St. Paul. Yes. St. Paul. It's all there."

William Brewster Nickerson

❧

Cape Cod tourist brochure referring to the Nickerson Room in a Chatham library asks rhetorically, "Who was W. B. Nickerson?" The answer gives the obituary particulars, born in 1942 and so on, and recommends the archives to visitors interested in local lore. William Brewster Nickerson, for whom the room was named, was named in turn for a direct antecedent who founded Chatham in Massachusetts in 1664 after buying the land from Mattaquason, the sachem of the Monomoyick tribe, in exchange for a small boat.

William was never anything but Bruce, already the Big Man on Campus, to all of us freshmen when we arrived at Dartmouth in 1961. He had prepared for college at Deerfield Academy and, exercising the privilege of an upperclassman, class of 1964, he roared into town in a 1955 MG TF-1500 roadster convertible, painted Dartmouth Green, a color called British Racing Green beyond the pale of the college. Even then it was something of a vintage item.

Bruce had been born on St. Patrick's Day, without the slightest claim to Celtic culture. He was not loathe to think of himself as a White Anglo-Saxon Protestant and, when the term was just coming into the vernacular, the green New Hampshire license plate on his MG read in white letters: WASP. (A decade later I would come to know Digby Baltzell, the University of Pennsylvania sociologist who routinely denied that he had invented the term universally ascribed to him, his objection being that White Anglo-Saxon is tautological in a slovenly manner.)

At some solemn moment one day, like the orderly and uncontested accession of a prince from coronet to crown, Bruce appeared without comment in the white shoes, trousers, cardigan, and cap of the president of the most revered secret society, Paleopitus, which carried with it the right to advise the president of the college on matters about which the president, in terms vaguely expressed, wanted to be advised. The only advice I remember Bruce giving was through a megaphone at football games, calling on us to insult Yale. He plowed into philosophy even though it was not his natural gift, finally confiding to me that the faculty told him that his written examination for graduation had given them a good laugh. Risibility has long been a subject of interest to sophists.

I had seen no serious side to Bruce, although in his elderly early twenties he was avuncular to one who was the youngest in the college and saved me from more than one faux pas. We tolerated President John Sloan Dickey's warning that our world was changing in strange ways. Each Monday night we were required to attend, in jacket and tie, Great Issues speeches by visitors unknown to us, like Malcolm X and Martin Luther King Jr. At Evensong in chapel, Bruce would indicate his preference for certain hymns by singing them loudly, so when he told me he

wanted to be a priest I consigned it to the attic of his passing enthusiasms.

First he'd do his navy duty, as the ROTC had been one
of his catalogue of campus activities. The bright green
MG was sold, as it would be of no use in Vietnam. He
summoned me before graduation and gave me the license
plate emblazoned WASP. I shook his hand and wished him
a thrilling time, and made no mention of the fact that he
was weeping as he said that he truly believed in God. He
was assigned to Attack Squadron 85 onboard the USS
Kitty Hawk, and on April 22, 1966, age twenty-four, he
flew as bombardier/navigator on a combat reconnaissance
mission near the city of Vinh in Ha Tinh Province. His
aircraft crashed about five miles offshore, and no remains
were recovered. I have his license plate next to my books of
the philosophers we once had read.

Walter Ciszek

꙾

efore there was an Armistice Day, Walter Ciszek was born on November II, 1904, and lived through a crucified century. Death came gracefully in 1984 on the feast of the Immaculate Conception. In boyhood he was a bully in a gang on the gritty streets of Shenandoah, Pennsylvania, and Ciszek's Polish immigrant father dragged him to the police station, hoping to put him into a reform school. Everyone thought he was joking when the eighth-grader announced that he would enter the Polish minor seminary. The seminarian swam in an icy lake and rose before dawn to run five miles, pummeling the body like his forebear in holy belligerence, Saul of Tarsus. A biography of St. Stanislaus Kostka inspired him to go to the Bronx in 1928, where he told the Jesuits he wanted to join up.

Guileless Ciszek then informed his superiors that God wanted him to go to Russia, where in ten years more than 150,000 Russian Orthodox priests had been wiped out. They sent him to study in Rome at the Russicum, the Jesuit's Russian center, and finally in 1937 he celebrated his first Mass in the Byzantine rite. Aiming to infiltrate Russia through Poland, he taught ethics in a seminary in

Albertyn. But in 1939 Hitler invaded from the west and then the Russians came from the east, despoiling the seminary, and so the young *alter Christus* was on the cross between two thieves. In 1940 the Ukrainian Archbishop of Lvov permitted him to enter Russia, and he headed for the Ural Mountains, a two-week trip in a box car with twenty-five men. While hauling logs in a lumber camp, he said Mass furtively in the forest. Secret police arrested him as a Vatican spy when they found his Mass wine, which they called nitroglycerine, and kept him in a cell 900 feet square for two weeks with 100 other men.

After six more months, beaten with rubber truncheons, starved, and drugged, he signed a confession, and this he called one of the darkest moments of his life. On July 26, 1942, he was sentenced to fifteen years hard labor, starting with five years of solitary confinement in Moscow's hideous Lubyanka prison, and then off to Siberia. After a slow 2,500-mile trip to Krasnoyarsk in a sweltering boxcar, he was sent on a barge to Norilsk, 200 miles north of the Arctic Circle, and worked twelve-hour days shoveling coal into freighters, with rags for shoes. In hushed tones he said Mass for Polish prisoners using a vodka glass for a chalice and wine made from stolen raisins. Having been transferred to work in the coal mines for a year, he became a construction worker in 1947, returning to the mines in 1953.

Release came in 1955 and he got news to his sisters for the first time since 1939 that he was alive. In Krasnoyarsk he quickly established several parishes. Then came four years just south in Abakan, working as an auto mechanic. In 1963 the KGB hauled him back to Moscow and handed him over to the American consulate in exchange for two

Soviet agents. As the plane flew past the Kremlin, he related, "slowly, carefully, I made the sign of the cross over the land that I was leaving."

In New York, undeterred by arthritis and cardiac ailments, he gave spiritual direction at Fordham University in a residence now named for him, writing his monumental books *With God in Russia* and *He Leadeth Me*. One summer day I was driven by some parish teenagers to a barbeque with him in New Rochelle. We arrived in the quiet suburban neighborhood in a noisily combustive van painted in psychedelic designs, used by the boys for their rock band. My last sight of him was in the garden, bouncing a small girl on his knee. His hair was very white and his radiance was not of the summer sun. "These are they which came out of great tribulation, and have washed their robes, and made them white in the blood of the Lamb" (Rv 7:14).

George Charles Lang

❧

By providence, George Charles Lang was named for the patron of soldiers in Flushing, New York, 1947, and soon his family moved to Hicksville out on Long Island where he began the battle that mankind, for want of a larger vocabulary, calls life. In *Tremendous Trifles*, Chesterton says that a baby's acquaintance with the dragon is not taught by fairy tales. It is intuitive of something that slithered in and shook Eden. What the fairy tale provides for him is a St. George to kill the dragon.

George was seven years old when his father died, and as soon as he was able he helped to support his mother by working long days in a luncheonette. After high school he enlisted in the army at Brooklyn, laden with the benisons of his parish, and soon was in search-and-destroy missions along the Mekong River.

In 1969, after six-months duty as a specialist fourth class, he was made a squad leader in Company A, 4th Battalion, 47th Infantry, 9th Infantry Division. His officer forgot to put in his date for rest and recreation, and on the birthday of another George (Washington), he was leading men through the mud in the spit-shined new shoes he got for his leave. On his first foray he single-handedly destroyed two enemy bunker complexes with grenades and rifle fire, hurling the last of the grenades he had found in an enemy cache. As he jumped across a canal to within a few feet of the enemy, his troops suffered six casualties in an ensuing onslaught of rockets and automatic-weapon fire from a third bunker. One rocket severed his spinal chord, but he continued to shout maneuvers in blinding pain. By the time he was evacuated against his protests he had secured the safety of his squad. In all, his tour of duty in Vietnam was less than a year.

For thirty-five years, George was a paraplegic. Two years after that fiery day, in the name of Congress, President Nixon awarded him the Medal of Honor. More sustained than his valor in Kien Hoa was the courage of his ensuing peace. Dryden said that peace itself is war in masquerade. In George's masquerade there were outward emoluments and honors, but the struggle of faith was interior, evidence of St. Ambrose's commentary on Psalm 118 that faith means battles. In 1973 he married Jacqueline and reared a step-daughter. Modestly did he do bookkeeping for a brother-in-law's company, which made strings for guitars, trying to fathom how he had been, to paraphrase his words, a hero who was not a hero, while painstakingly dictating much of a two-volume history of Medal of Honor recipients. At Mass, he regularly received the Host on the tongue as he had as a boy, all the while aware of God's heroes called saints who are an exceedingly great army. Shredded as he had been by enemy fire, irony killed him in 2005 with cancer and not bullets or rockets.

A few months before, he appeared at a benefit dinner in natty formal dress with the light blue ribbon of the

Congressional Medal, which gives me pause like nothing save the Blessed Sacrament. When I spoke with him of Rev. Vincent Capodanno, Maryknoll priest and Marine chaplain, who was awarded the Medal of Honor after dying in 1967 while giving last rites, George was so animated I thought he might rise from his wheelchair, so keen was he on efforts to promote Father Capodanno's cause for sainthood. Flags filled the streets for George Lang's funeral Mass. The Medal of Honor was displayed, and there was a medal of St. George. The last funeral he had watched was President Reagan's, and he had been moved by a new hymn sung on that day:

> To fallen soldiers let us sing,
> Where no rockets fly nor bullets wing,
> Our broken brothers let us bring
> To the Mansions of the Lord.

Elizabeth Windsor

❧

She was the only woman I knew who lived in three centuries, and was the longest-lived English royal when she died on Easter Eve in 2002—a record until her sister-in-law, the Duchess of Gloucester, died at 102. But as do all the children of Adam, she began young, and nursed the wounded in the Great War, which took the life of her brother Fergus.

Growing up with nine siblings in the Scottish castle of Glamis in Angus, her Jacobite bloodlines never yielded to Calvinism. While circumstances of state blocked roads to Rome, as Queen Mother she restored Canova's memorial to the Stuart kings in St. Peter's Basilica, and the apostolic pro-nuncio frequently cooked dinner for her in his residence. The royal eye gazed upon priestesses in the Established Church as physical and metaphysical absurdities.

Lady Elizabeth Bowes-Lyon first shunned marriage to the Duke of York: "Afraid never, never again to be free to think, speak and act as I feel I really ought to." (She never did make a public speech until her 100th birthday.) Queen Mary lumbered in on her son's behalf like a bejeweled mastodon, and Elizabeth yielded to the shy, stammering man whose death she would mourn painfully. At the wedding in Westminster Abbey, she placed her bouquet on the grave of the Unknown Soldier, evoking what her father-in-law's ambassador to Washington wrote for choral rafters: "I vow to thee, my country, all earthly things above, / Entire and whole and perfect, the service of my love. . . . "

Let none gainsay the last Queen Empress the benefactions of an empire covering twenty percent of the world's land surface and one-quarter of the human race who were in her nightly litany. The imperial sunset flushed her quiet disapprobation of Lord Mountbatten's plans for India. Cold highland hours in trout streams were respite from the lifelong treadmill of public events in crinolines and ostrich feathers, always smiling through migraines and aching feet. *Memento mori* was a grand protocol, and each year her funeral was rehearsed and filmed, with horses in the mock cortege. Drinks flowed as she and the chamberlains fine-tuned anthems for a proper walk through the valley of the shadow of death.

If the Edwardian lady without an Edwardian hourglass figure resembled an amiable pudding, Hitler called her the most dangerous woman in Europe, and she kept a pistol in her purse, ready for an invasion. In later years came elegant vagueness. When Princess Illeana of Romania, who had become an Orthodox nun, came to breakfast, she thought she was the Queen of Holland. With more than fifty personal servants to the last, her virtues did not include domestic economies.

I was first presented to her at Clarence House in 1967 by Churchill's daughter Mary Soames, whose loveliness, though a remote radiance in the perspective of my youth, dazzled me out of adolescence. On another occasion, we had tea with a sour Krishna Menon who had been voted out of the Indian parliament and did not share the tradition of smiling come what may. At Clarence House, those of my age were given sherry by the same footman who served the queen gin. Standing by a bed of camellias she told me to look up, and soon hovering over us was a purple helicopter with Margaret flashing a beacon to Mother.

More than a million attended her funeral, and in repose she played her part well. Almost eighty years after her wedding the flowers from her coffin were removed and placed on the grave of the Unknown Soldier.

And there's another country, I've heard of long ago,
Most dear to them that love her, most great to them
    that know;
We may not count her armies, we may not see her King;
Her fortress is a faithful heart, her pride is suffering;
And soul by soul and silently her shining bounds
    increase,
And her ways are ways of gentleness, and all her paths
    are peace.

Eugen Rosenstock-Huessy

꙳

A s 1978 was the Year of the Three Popes, so was 1888 the Year of the Three Emperors: Drei Achten, drei Kaiser. Eugen Rosenstock was born to Jewish parents in the three eights of Wilhelm I, Frederick III, and Wilhelm II. He studied law at Zurich, Heidelberg, and Berlin and shone in Leipzig as the youngest law professor in all Germany. The death of his father impelled him into banking to support his family, and soon he joined the Berlin Stock Exchange.

The family's eclectic religious perspective did not disdain his baptism as a Protestant when he was eighteen. As World War I loomed, he married Margrit Huessy, a Swiss student of art history whom he met in Florence; and then, as a lieutenant in the mounted artillery, he fought for eighteen months in the cauldron of Verdun. Between gas attacks he taught the troops linguistics and rudimentary philosophy. Why not? C. S. Lewis invoked those who discuss the last new poem while advancing to the walls of Quebec, and comb their hair at Thermopylae. There has been published from that barbaric time his civilized correspondence with the Jewish philosopher Franz Rosenzweig, Eugen having become a Christian. His book of 1920, *The Marriage of War and Revolution*, warned of social horrors to come.

The polymath won a second doctorate in 1923 from Heidelberg for medieval studies, all the while conducting night schools for factory workers and fighting off the seductions of Marxists who looked upon him as a prize catch. Volumes poured forth on social analysis using philology as a matrix, a system he called metanomics. Christ the Word is known by speech, not logic. A lectureship in social science in Darmstadt led to a full professorship in legal history at Breslau, a base for organizing the Lowensberger *arbeitslager* to reform the appalling conditions in the Silesian coal mines. It would become a center of anti-Nazi resistance.

An officer of Daimler-Benz helped him edit the first factory newspaper in Germany, a remote prototype of the encyclical *Laborem Exercens*, written by a former chemical factory worker. To expose the anemia of idealism and positivism modish in the dispirited post-war universities, he published *Die Kreatur*, a journal edited by a Jew, Martin Buber, a Protestant, von Weizsacker, and a Catholic priest, Wittig, whom he would later defend against excommunication. In 1931, the gigantic *European Revolutions and the Character of Nations* showed how the Great War had ended the progress of Christian civilization in Europe rooted in five national revolutions.

After the birth of a son, Hans, and in 1933 exile to the United States from the Nazis, he adopted his hyphenated name and landed as a lecturer at Harvard, where his Christianity was disdained in arched tones as blatant as the bugles of the National Socialists. Gracefully, he became a professor of social philosophy at Dartmouth, where he taught until 1957 and lived until 1973. I knew him as a revered retired presence, more vocal in praying in the chapel than emoting on the crisis of mankind. He lived across the river in Vermont, where he had formed a Civilian Conservation Corps in 1940 at the behest of President Roosevelt, enlisting students from Dartmouth, Radcliffe, and Harvard. Forty books and 500 essays later, with many converts to his credit, the widower was cared for by the widow of the executed resistance leader Count von Moltke, who had been formed in the Lowensberger student camps.

One day Rosenstock-Huessy waited for his old friend Martin Buber in White River Junction, the railroad station closest to our campus. They embraced and wept. And in that moment, a faded New England train stop became Jerusalem and Rome and the Heavenly City where they sing the song of Moses the servant of God, and the song of the Lamb.

Jesus Vasquez

※

s I was unfamiliar with the Spanish convention of
naming boys for the Savior, it startled me upon arriving in my new parish to read on the bulletin board:
If there is no usher at the 7:30 Mass, Jesus will take up
the collection. So I came under the tutelage of sexton
Jesus Vasquez (1927–1996), a prototype and amalga-
mation of all the church sextons who would rather be a
doorkeeper in the house of their Lord than dwell in the
tents of ungodliness.

This husband of a quiet wife and father of six children,
who reciprocated his adoration of them, sustained them
on a small income with no apparent astringency of domestic manners. He was equally ebullient with his extended
family of the many saints whose statues he dusted daily,
sometimes with groanings that could indeed be uttered,
especially when taking up issues with Martin de Porres,
whose statue he resembled.

As one tried in the fire, he arrived in the United States
after being urged to leave the Dominican Republic for having been a student agitator while in medical school. When
he abandoned hope of a professional career, he retained

the classical culture in which he had been formed and grimaced if a clergyman mangled Latin. Other times he would peer from the sacristy door at a liturgical faux pas with a pained look freighted with all of the agonies of the Church's suffering since guitarists and skirted dancers broke down the gates of the sanctuary.

For this Jesus, a high feast was the annual anniversary of his new citizenship. When he was semi-comatose on his deathbed, he recited the Pledge of Allegiance in the English he had laboriously studied in night school. In turn, he taught me much Castellano, explaining that my Spanish tutor was teaching me expressions useful only if I had been summoned to the court of Alfonso XIII.

Politely unspoken condescension marked his face whenever I suggested some change in the daily routine, for of that routine he was master, and on more than one occasion he would summon the priest to rejoice in the dawn if he had not heard the alarm for Angelus. This Jesus had no power to call the dead forth from their tombs, but he could weep as did Jesus in Bethany, often when he functioned as a sort of professional mourner at the funerals of people who had no one to keep vigil over their bodies. As a coffin was carried out onto the busy street, he managed to toll the tower bell once for each year of the departed life, and still be on the curb with hat off and head bowed for the final blessing. It was close to bilocation, and I never asked how he managed it.

A sturdy build served him well when he hammer-locked a pickpocket and dragged him from the pew to the street with an inconspicuous grace that did not interrupt the Gloria. He spied a thief carrying off my chalice as I was greeting people at the door after Mass and he leaped after him like a gazelle, knocked him to the ground, and pried the precious cup from the menacing hands. On busy days he would choreograph the confessional lines, and I feared that he might start dividing the mortals from the venials. Having been a serious amateur boxer, he was full of advice but bemused when I started boxing lessons, clearly perplexed by someone making a sport of what was for him almost a necessity: he lived in a neighborhood where the manly art of self-defense really was for self-defense. He was shot in the leg during some random violence near his home, and was back on the job as soon as he got out of the hospital. "I do not run aimlessly, nor do I box as though beating the air; but I punish my body and enslave it, so that after proclaiming to others I myself should not be disqualified" (I Cor 9:26–27).

William F. Burke Jr.

❧

f wag said that calling Billy Burke a fireman was like calling Elvis an entertainer. The Requiem Mass in St. Patrick's Cathedral for Captain William F. Burke Jr. (1955–2001) at which I was celebrant and preacher was the biggest funeral I ever had. The cardinal presided from the throne, and present were a governor, mayor, and United Nations secretary general. Thousands stood outside on Fifth Avenue, but there was no coffin and no corpse, for Billy was crushed and incinerated in Tower Two of the World Trade Center. I had watched it collapse in a sickening sort of slow motion, and yet I wandered in shock through the smoke trying to see it, for I could not morally register what my retinas had recorded.

Billy of Engine Company 21 was the most decorated fire captain in the city and in the headlines many times, having rescued infants from fires in a life that was the stuff of melodrama. He was one of six children born to a deputy fire chief in the South Bronx, and he wanted to be like his father, who fought blaze after blaze in the 1960s when his precinct was like a war zone. He also spent twenty-five summers as a lifeguard at Robert Moses State Park, where there is a memorial to him. To fulfill the dying wish of the park's oldest living lifeguard, Billy lifted him out of his wheelchair and carried him into the waves for one last swim. He liked to say, "I'm a [delete] hero."

He died on September 11 helping another man in a wheelchair. Having evacuated all of his men and thousands of civilians, he found Edward Beyea, a quadriplegic, on the twenty-seventh floor with a coworker, Abe Zelmanowitz, who would not leave him unattended, and the captain would leave neither of them. He telephoned a friend at 10:15 who begged him to get out, and he told her, "This is my job. This is who I am." Fourteen minutes later, the tower fell down.

Billy's friends were legion, and in their ranks were women who found him charming enough to get him named among the city's more eligible bachelors, a *bon vivant* with none of the boulevardier's cynicism and a gallant with none of Lothario's concomitant enormities. Among his loves was military history; he visited Gettysburg five times and took one young lady on their first date to Grant's Tomb. The autodidact became a writer, chef, and painter. A piano filled much of the space in his small apartment in Stuyvesant Town. His faith was blunt and cheerful, and priests whose virtue he exaggerated discerned in him a priestliness that might have brought him to ordination but in a division of labor, he let them save souls from the fires of hell while he saved them from the fires of tenements.

As I stood in the pulpit at the captain's funeral, the acoustics were tried in a singular way, for I had never before preached against such a wave of weeping, nor had I faced so many thousands of sad eyes; but the object of our

suffrages would have been bemused at the many children
in the street wearing Captain Billy memorial T-shirts. At
the end of the rites, so many public officials said a few
words that there went out a wise decree banning gratuitous
eulogies in the archdiocese.

On an Internet web site where people condoled, one
wrote: "I feel deep pain for his family but yet great joy
because he is now with God." Some sectarian of the dour
sort whose vocation is to remind us that this is a vale of
tears immediately replied, "He's not with God, he's sleeping,
awaiting the second coming. Look in Ecclesiastes 9:5 and
I Thessalonians 4:16." Billy Burke, who believed in purgatory, would have thought that imprecise. A survivor whom
he rescued before going back into the tower recalled, "I
turned around, and he wasn't there." There are those who
said the same thing on the first Easter.

Maria Cristina Marconi

꙯

"Most Holy Father, the work that Your Holiness has deigned to entrust to me, I today return to You. . . . May you deign, Holy Father, to allow the entire world to hear your august words," Guglielmo Marconi beseeched Pius XI at the inauguration of the Vatican Radio in 1931, thirty-six years after he sent a wireless signal one-and-a-half miles from his father's country estate in Pontecchio. On many occasions, his widow, the Marchesa Maria Cristina (1900–1994), served me wine from the vineyard on that property. She was twenty-six years younger than he when they wed, having met on his 730-ton, 220-foot-long yacht, the *Elettra*, which functioned as a floating laboratory. A large model of it was encased in her entrance hall, long after it had been requisitioned by the Germans in Trieste and torpedoed by a British submarine off the Dalmation coast in 1944.

The marchesa spoke of her husband, born in Bologna, as Scottish, and indeed, his early childhood was in Ireland, after which his schoolmates in Florence mocked his poor Italian. He was reared as an Anglican. When my parents visited the marchesa in the Palazzo Maruscelli on the Via

Condotti, she, not innocent of eugenics, allowed that my mother's English bloodline and my father's French were the two best. In the belief that Americans drink only whiskey and sherry, she kindly poured both in large water glasses filled to the brim.

Guglielmo's first marriage was to a daughter of the fourteenth Baron Inchiquin of Ireland. He did not revere all the Mosaic commandments in equal measure, and there was a messy divorce in 1924. Maria Cristina Bezzi-Scali, of the Black Nobility, lovingly tamed him, and he embraced Catholicism, marrying her in 1927 after an annulment. I thought of the faith that by God's grace I helped to light and keep burning more and more brightly in his soul. . . . The birth of a daughter, the future Princess Elettra (named for the yacht), when he was fifty-six made him a doting family man.

One afternoon the marchesa showed me a family film in which, for one brief moment, I recognized Mussolini boarding their yacht. He had been best man at their wedding, and in 1930 the great inventor joined the Fascist Grand Council. For defending the invasion of Ethiopia, he was banned from the airwaves of the BBC that he had helped create. When he died suddenly at the age of sixty-three, dressing for an appointment with the Duce, all the radio stations in the world kept two minutes of silence. Italian fascism was a sensitive subject, although the devout marchesa was hostile to the Nazis. In a weekly political arabesque, the German high commander in Rome would arrive for tea, which was served to him, and then she would withdraw, leaving him on his own. She kept the chair Monsignor Pacelli used when he taught her the catechism. She did not mourn Paul VI, who abolished the papal nobility while she was abroad, and she also thought little of David Sarnoff, whom her husband got started, for his false claims of receiving the Titanic's radio messages.

The marchesa became grandmotherly when she asked a friend and me to translate her memoirs. I was unable to bring them to print. The wife of the publisher, Bennett Cerf, thought the serene widow's fondness for details of wardrobe overwhelmed historic encounters. Her daughter happily produced an edition in 1999.

Once running a *marathonina* I thought I might not make it to the finish line on the Capitoline Hill, but as I ran down the Corso, the Marchesa Marconi and the Principessa Elettra were there as they had promised, cheering loudly, and I finished the race. In the college chapel that night the Vespers lection was from I Corinthians, written by one who became a Roman by death: "So run that ye may obtain."

Robert Francis Wilberforce

❧

I t was through his brother-in-law, Louis Bancel Warren, that I got to know Robert Francis Wilberforce (1887–1988), and none too soon, for he was closing in on his 100th birthday—a genetic habit of the family, for his mother died in her 100th year, and his father was ninety-one in a time of rudimentary medicine. Louis and his sister were descendants of the American Revolutionary War general Philip Schuyler; and in Oxford at Balliol, Louis had become fast friends with Robert (generally known as Bath Bob because of his association with that ancient spa, the Anglo-Saxon Venice).

Bath Bob married Hope Elizabeth Warren, author of a book on Persian rugs, of which she had many, three days after the assassination of Archduke Ferdinand and the change of the world. During the Great War he worked with the War Trade Intelligence Department and was an attaché of His Majesty's Legation to the Holy See. As a prominent English Catholic he tried hard to convince the Vatican that Catholicism in England was not an exotic orchid, while also representing to the Crown that the armada and Gunpowder Plot were long past. He wrote from Rome in 1918 to the novelist Shane Leslie: "Great changes have taken place here during the last year in views and prejudices at headquarters. The realization of the Anglo-Saxon element in Catholicism and its loyalty to the Holy See is growing strong. Everyone is looking West now. . . . "

He was a great-grandson of the Liberator, William Wilberforce. In 1814 Madame de Staël was surprised that the most religious man in England was also the wittiest man in England, and Bath Bob inherited much of that spark. The family was of Wilberfoss in Yorkshire, tracing itself to the Saxon Ulgar of Eggleston, whose father fought in 1066 at Stanford Bridge. Grandfather Henry became a Catholic as an unanticipated consequence of the Oxford Movement and edited the *Catholic Standard.* He had married a sister of Emily Sargent, wife of the Anglican bishop of Oxford, Samuel Wilberforce. Soapy Sam was famous for his frail debate with Huxley on Darwinism. Yet another daughter of the Rev. John Sargent of Lavington was married to an Anglican archdeacon later known as Cardinal Manning, and so Bath Bob liked to say that he was the cardinal's great-nephew. Bob's grandfather Henry and another great-uncle, Robert, had been close friends of Newman at Oriel College, where Newman told Henry that there is no medium between Pantheism and the Church of Rome. His grandson told me that during a typhoid epidemic Henry and his wife nursed dying immigrant Irish hops pickers, and his grandfather was sure that their final blessings had greased his slide into Catholicism.

After the Great War, Bob directed the British Library of Information in New York, undertook several diplomatic missions, and became a barrister-at-law in the Inner

Temple. As his branch of Wilberforces reveled in the ancient Faith, his father studied at the Oratory School under Newman and at Stonyhurst. Before going on to Balliol, Bob was educated in turn at Beaumont College in Old Windsor. Years before that, while he was not yet three years old, his father took him to see John Henry Cardinal Newman, months before the cardinal's final illness in 1890. "At so early an age I did not appreciate the significance of the man, but I remember him arriving in a carriage and being helped up the steps, all in red. The priest assisting him was Father Neville, and I have a volume of *Verses on Various Occasions* inscribed by Newman to him." But in Bath Bob I knew probably the last living person actually to have heard the Voice that Matthew Arnold remembered breaking the silence with words and thoughts which were religious music—subtle, sweet, mournful. . . .

Austin Vaughan

❧

Preparing for my priestly ordination, Bishop Austin Vaughan (1927–2000) conferred the ministries of lector and acolyte with such unassuming dispatch that one forgot the man was possibly the smartest bishop in the nation. Nothing seemed quite to fit him; he appeared not so much to be dressed as to be in the process of dressing, and the mitre sat askew on top the elegant brain. Since student days in Rome, rumors followed him that he had scored the finest academic record since St. Alphonsus Liguori dazzled his examiners. An eclectic curriculum vitae listed presidencies of the Catholic Theological Society and the Mariological Society, as well as vicariate of the prison apostolate for which he had distinguished credentials as the first bishop of the land to have been arrested nobly. Our jaded judiciary found him flawed by statute, and judges sentenced him many times for protesting outside abortion clinics. "I've been in some of the best jails in the country." He would fall limp and make it difficult for the police to haul his frame into the wagon, but as an inmate with a rosary he charmed convicts and shamed guards.

During two vacancies in New York it is believed that he was consulted about accepting the archbishopric, from which he demurred as a bad organizer. He had done the same when he was rector of the archdiocesan seminary. Cardinal Cooke persisted and made him auxiliary bishop in 1977. As vicar for Orange County and a pastor in Newburgh, he was *maitre d'hotel* of a four-star soup kitchen and, among many unpublicized acts, housed and boarded a score of refugees from an apartment building fire. The Latinist ministered to his flock in five languages, including a dash of Polish.

There must have been pain when he resigned his allegiance to the Democratic Party in 1988—"the party of abortion," as he put it in an open letter that rebuked Gov. Mario Cuomo, who claimed that Vatican II had done away with hell. More hurtful was the opprobrium he endured as seminary rector in his defense of the articles of *Humanae Vitae* in 1968, and worldwide travels in support of Paul VI were his yin to the yang of the pope's subsequent agonized silence. The bishop's material poverty was a radical instinct, and it took a moral dimension when he was neglected by many he had counted as colleagues.

Vaughan understood that not every meeting is or should be Nicaea, and even a bishop's conference can bounce between platitude and error. True to his prediction, lengthy and heady national pastoral letters on economics and war and peace that danced on the grave of reason are relegated now to the cabinet of failed curiosities. Metastasized bureaucracies, even clerical ones, risk becoming bottom feeders of culture if they conjoin inanity, which has no cure, and cupidity, which shrinks from cure. In that ecology disquieted by precise thought and courage, the prophet is a pest.

Only once in my presence did he marvel, ever so gently, that successors to the apostles could be in communion with Peter but not in empathy with Peter. That scandal may have been his hardest mortification. One triumph over committees was to thwart a defective translation of a book of prayers, delivering a critique to each bishop before the day of voting, but in consequence he was patronized as an eccentric by the self-centered.

The lustrous mind and unflagging frame endured the final humiliation of a long, speechless infirmity from a stroke, and when he could no longer say Mass he made himself an altar of sacrifice. Among his few possessions was a letter of support written to him in prison by another fine theologian named Joseph Ratzinger, and a higher power arranged that he be buried on the feast of Sts. Peter and Paul, which had been the day of his ordination as a bishop.

Jerome Hines

✣

"We are facing a generation of young singers who are much more diminutive in their approach to singing." There was nothing diminutive about the man who said that. Jerome Hines (1921–2003) stood six-feet, six-inches tall, and on stage at La Scala in 1968 as Handel's Hercules, the hero seemed an eponym for himself. His pinnacle was to sing Boris Godunov in Moscow at the Bolshoi, but his real triumph was mentioning Christ to the Soviet secret police and smuggling bibles into the Kremlin.

He began as Heinz, but Sol Hurok changed the spelling around the time of his debut in *Rigoletto* with the San Francisco Opera in 1941, because of the German problem. It did not prevent him from singing as King Mark and Wotan and Gurnemanz at Bayreuth in a happier time in the late 1950s. It was around then that my father took me to hear Lauritz Melchior in New York, not so much for Wagner as for the fact that he looked so much like my Grandpa, who had just died and who had sung as a student in Lyons. The *heldentenor* Melchior and *basso* Hines defined opera for me.

The evangelical conversion of Hines was quite a turn-around from his youth, but even his socializing had a theme. Dating Patrice Munsel, "our conversations usually ended up sounding like vocal master-classes." He became a master teacher himself, writing two coaching books, *Great Singers on Great Singing* and *The Four Voices of Man*. After his Met debut in 1946, he turned down a ten-year contract there because he thought some of the avant-garde choreography was too suggestive, but in spite of cancer and arthritis he set the all-time record for the Met: 868 performances in forty-one seasons.

The same man who was unsurpassed as Mephistoph-eles, the assassin Sparafucile, and the Grand Inquisitor, played Christ in the opera he composed: *I Am the Way*. On the Met stage he looked like Sallman's painting of "The Head of Christ" come to life. Rampant guilelessness moved this singer, who ranged from Verdi to Stravinsky, to name his autobiography *This Is My Story, This Is My Song*, from the words of the hymn written in 1873 by Fanny Crosby, who probably thought Sir Arthur Sullivan a bit risqué. Without straining convention, I can say I detected in him not the slightest censoriousness of broken virtue. Even once when I egged him on to say something quotable about Gigli's weepy tremolo, he remarked how devoted Gigli had been to one of his legitimate daughters, the soprano Rina. Gigli's confessor was Padre Pio, a circum-stance the born-again Hines might have found alien to his own instincts but salutary.

My introduction to him was by way of the pro-life movement. He told me that, years before, one of his four sons was expected to be born with Down Syndrome, and he and his wife chose to be stewards of the life the Creator allowed them to procreate. The challenge became a gift. Once when an argument disrupted the family dinner, the young boy, confused by the commotion, got up from the table and kissed his mother and father and brothers and sat down. All fell silent and there was peace. Once we sat together at a fundraiser in New Jersey listening to a valiant young woman sing "God Bless America." She was less than half his great height, as she had been born with multiple birth defects. He whispered with tears that he had never heard such a glorious voice.

Mrs. Hines, aptly named Lucia Evangelista, also sang in the opera. When Lou Gehrig's Disease paralyzed her voice and body, Hines tended her for many years, often bringing guests in to watch a film of her in *La Traviata*. He promised to follow her soon, hoping to see Jesus, and so he did, not long after singing one last time with the Boston Bel Canto Opera, aged nearly eighty.

Richard Conway Casey

❧

After nearly forty years as a lawyer, Richard Conway Casey (1933–2006) was sworn in as a judge of the U.S. district court in Manhattan in 1977. Following Holy Cross and Georgetown, he had been a soldier and a legal investigator for the New York County district attorney's office and an assistant U.S. attorney, specializing in public corruption cases. When the Catholic lawyers of New York dedicated a shrine to St. Thomas More in my church, he was there with his guide dog, Barney. The retinitis pigmentosa, which had been diagnosed in 1964, led to complete blindness in 1987.

"When I became blind, I didn't know a single individual who was blind. I didn't know if you just sat there and waited to die, or what you did. You're facing life and what appears to be a grim future. The one thing you have is faith." His confirmation as the first blind federal trial judge in the nation followed a challenge in the Senate hearing. He reminded the Judiciary Committee that if justice is blind, a blind judge would not be at a disadvantage. There were problems physical, if not philosophical: On his first day on the bench, he walked into a wall. Eventually he mastered an optic scanner with synthetic voice, learned how to ski, and taught blind children the sport.

In 2004 he agonized over a decision on a technical point to rule against the Partial-Birth Abortion Ban Act, but his questioning of witnesses over sixteen days was as monumental as any *obiter dictum* at the Nuremburg trials. In redirect examination of one abortionist, he challenged euphemisms such as decompression of the skull and reducing the contents of the skull. He asked if a fetus feels pain. When the doctor replied that it never crossed his mind, the judge asked, "Never?" and gave the nation opportunity to hear the cold reply: "No." He recalled how the abortionists did not tell the women in simple language that "what you're doing is tearing the arms and legs off the body." Constitutional restraints did not prevent his declaration that partial-birth abortion is a gruesome, brutal, barbaric, and uncivilized medical procedure. The final judgment was a Pyrrhic victory for the technicians, for judicial history will remember their silence in the courtroom when Casey asked what they would tell a mother to do if they knew her unborn child would be blind.

At one banquet of the Order of Malta, which he served as president of the American Association, he introduced from memory the twenty or so guests assembled on the dais. My last time seated with him was at a right-to-life dinner when my only help to him was to tell him that the vegetable on his plate was at three o'clock and the meat was a quarter to twelve. But at his wake I was asked to read one of his order's prayers, with some of his fellow knights and his dog Barney guarding his coffin. Afterward, a gentleman expressed to me his sense that the prayer's reference to enemies of religion was archaic in our tolerant society. That refined ignorance was not unfamiliar to Richard Casey, nor was it unknown to his patron Thomas More, and it was the ground of their mutual humor and sorrow.

In 1999, Pope John Paul II received him when he was awarded the Blessed Hyacinthe Cormier Medal at the Angelicum University for outstanding leadership in the promotion of gospel values in the field of justice and ethics. He remembered going to Lourdes when he went blind and being led to the grave of an atheist Italian girl who had been brought against her wishes to the shrine for a cure. She remained blind in eye, but was transfigured in spirit. As an old lady, she had asked to be buried near the spot where the Lady had appeared to Bernadette. The epitaph read to him was: "What is important is not to see but to understand."

Bowie Kent Kuhn

※

As baseball fans religiously record statistics, Bowie Kent Kuhn (1926–2007) was, at forty-two, the youngest commissioner of baseball ever; the tallest, at six-foot-five; and the heaviest, at 250 pounds, though his height made him seem slim.

As I measured up to none of that, I was not an impressive guide when I led him and his wife, Luisa, through the woods of Colorado while on retreat. As snow began to fall, I imagined our becoming a sequel to the Donner party. Bowie appeared in many outdoor situations, including pro-life marches, but most famously was he in the bleachers adjudicating some of the rifest controversies in baseball history, overseeing the renaissance of the national pastime through the use of television for night games, and the expansion of the major leagues to twenty-six teams.

I do not think he ever wavered from an uncomplicated faith, and often he would ask me to hear his confession with the stolid practicality of a player donning his uniform for a double-header. In our various trips with Legatus, the organization of Catholic business leaders, he scheduled

the sacraments and prayer times as though he were making
calls from the dugout.

Baseball was like an organic appendage, and he chose his
first law firm of Willkie, Farr & Gallagher because it rep-
resented the National League. Some thought him morally
arch, as when he panned Jim Bouton's book *Ball Four* as detri-
mental to baseball. In 1985 Peter Ueberroth reinstated Wil-
lie Mays and Mickey Mantle to play after Bowie had banned
them for promoting gambling casinos. At dinner in the far
reaches of Long Island on August 14, 1995, the day after
Mantle died, Bowie listed for me the reasons he could not
in conscience attend the funeral. I thought it a fine parade
of righteous indignation in contradistinction to the self-
righteousness above which he stood aloof as philosophically
as physically. "My Church taught me the importance of
right and wrong. . . . The Church is my bulwark."

When Billy Martin, who accused Bowie of violating
basic rights of players, was given a gargantuan funeral after
a car crash in bibulous circumstances, and eulogized from
the pulpit as sliding into the heavenly home plate safe,
Bowie had no comment, but he wrote in his memoir, *Hard-
ball*, that Martin had a wryness that one would find in an
abused animal that precluded trust or affection. Suspend-
ing George Steinbrenner for making illegal campaign con-
tributions, and the same for Tiger's pitcher Denny McLain
for illegal bookmaking, were other testaments of Bowie's
discomfort with moral ambiguity. The man who had been
elected commissioner unanimously in 1969 on the first
ballot was eased out not all that easily by a coalition of
managers after the 1984 season.

Skills with which he promoted groups like the Catholic Values Investment Trust and a committee to defend the representation of the Holy See at the United Nations failed to rescue an ill-advised law partnership. It was another instance of his incongruity with others who preferred the shallows to the higher ground of ethics, and because of bankruptcy laws he moved from New Jersey to Florida, where an offended dignity continued to nurse AIDS patients and pursue philanthropy undeterred.

In Texas he told a convention how I had coded a combination lock in my rectory to match the date of the death of Pope St. Symmachus. For some reason he found my mnemonic device amusing, as did some 600 cowboys who, from that moment, were theoretically able to break into my dining room. A few days before his death, preparing for elective coronary surgery, he indicated to me on the telephone that Extreme Unction is a better strategy than stealing home.

William Liguori Nolan

❧

At the age of eight, the prodigy William Liguori Nolan (1916–2000) played the piano for Paderewski. He continued his studies at the Boston Latin School and outshone another musical classmate, his friend Leonard Bernstein. The class of 1935 elected their *wunderkind* its president and captain of the debate team.

Paderewski's heart has a gilded home in the National Shrine of Our Lady of Czestochowa in Pennsylvania. Nolan's heart was always in New Hampshire, where he loved living thirty-seven years as Catholic chaplain at Dartmouth. Paderewski went back to the piano after his premiership of Poland, but Father Nolan knew he had left the keyboard forever in 1943 when he was ordained a Redemptorist priest at Mount St. Alphonsus Seminary in Esopus, New York. For three years he taught homiletics and then, like his brother, preached missions around the country.

He prayerfully left his order to incardinate in the Diocese of Manchester, becoming a curate in the New Hampshire parish of St. Denis in Hanover. His pastor suspended him for providing a keg of beer to undergraduates, but the bishop, by a mystical intuition, cheerfully decided that Father Bill should become Catholic chaplain to the college in 1950.

Dartmouth then was as Anglo-Saxon Protestant as it was possible to be without casting anchor on the May-flower. In its remoteness, it was not traumatized during the revolution against King George III, who had granted its charter and for whom some of its sons kept fugitive sympathies. It was the only colonial college not to sus-pend commencement ceremonies during that confusion. Although its school color was green, it was not Irish green and certainly not Irish-Catholic green.

Nolan's establishment of an Aquinas House caused a minor tremor in the old-boy network, but President John Sloan Dickey, a man of vague Erastian philosophi-cal principles, befriended him. So began a chronology of youth shaped by his spiritual lights. And when the college became the last of the Ivies to admit students who were not male, he guided them, too. They now roam the girdled earth, taking their faith with them in all the arts and sci-ences. Some wear black and purple in the clergy; more than one skeptical student is now a professor of theology, and a granddaughter of General Patton is a Benedictine nun. But only he, always called Father Bill even after Paul VI made him a Prelate of Honor, could count them, as he kept pictures of them all.

A Baroque achievement in 1962 was the dedication of the Catholic Student Center at the end of Fraternity Row and within chanting distance of the president's house. Not a Catholic then myself, it was the first time I had seen a statue of Mary placed, inappropriately I thought at the time, over an altar.

For all his gentle dignity, Father Bill had the panache to place a stained-glass window of Cardinal Cushing next to Thomas Aquinas and John Henry Newman. Aquinas and Newman gave much from the treasury of saints, but Cushing gave negotiable currency. Father Bill told me how he was kept waiting for several hours in an antechamber of Sen. Edward Kennedy's office where he had gone to ask for help in completing the building, only to be dismissed as a bothersome acolyte. Of course, the senator, a Catholic, had attended an alien school to the south. Nelson Rockefeller, a Baptist of sorts but an alumnus, was a congenial font of munificence.

In 1973, the modern papist missionary was laurelled an honorary Doctor of Divinity by the institution founded by a Congregationalist missionary to the Indians of the northern wilds. Mr. Chips was a character in fiction, but as this real Mr. Chips died, he was able to see with eyes closed so many young faces pass by calling him "Father."

Jean-Marie Lustiger

❧

ournalists trying to assess the life of Jean-Marie
Lustiger (1926–2007) are like the crowd at the foot
of Mount Sinai trying to figure out why Moses was
complicating their lives. An eloquent sadness in him was
too ancient for any one race to claim; and when, in 1999,
he read his own mother's name, Gisele, at a public remembrance of deported and dead French Jews and added "ma
maman," he spoke with a voice older than Exodus, and as
old as the first day outside Eden.

His parents were non-practicing Ashkenazi Jews,
immigrants to France from Bendzin in Poland in the
First World War, and his father survived his mother in
Auschwitz in 1943. On a visit to Germany in 1937, he
stayed with an anti-Hitler family of Protestants and read
the New Testament for the first time. In 1940, his sister
joined him in converting to Christianity while under the
protection of a Catholic family in Orléans whose bishop
baptized Aaron, adding the names Jean-Marie. The pain
of losing his mother in such a crucible of evil ached all the
more from his father's sense of betrayal. Charles, who kept
a hosiery business, was of radical political views and held

the tradition of the generations his one vital link to moral cogency. When Jean-Marie was ordained a priest, Charles watched his son from the rear of the cathedral, and the beauty of heaven that can seem harsh on earth was there that hour.

His life from then on would be rattled by lesser men on every side for whom he was not enough of this or that. Charles had tried to get the chief rabbi of Paris to annul his son's baptism, and the *Jerusalem Post* announced his death with a headline calling him an apostate. In another quarter, the shadows of Maurras and Pétain lurked long. When Pope John Paul II named Parisian-born Lustiger archbishop of Paris in 1981, Archbishop Lefebvre publicly objected to the appointment of someone who was not truly of French origin.

Lustiger was a rabbinical clone of Wojtyla, who gave him the red hat in 1983. This was clear from his first Mass as Bishop of Orléans. His predecessor, Guy-Marie Riobe, had genuflected before every trend of the day, leaving the diocese a material and spiritual shambles, and Lustiger did not mention his name. At the Mass, when all the people joined in the conclusion of the Eucharistic Prayer as they had been recently taught to do, Lustiger firmly placed his hand on the altar and said, "This is mine."

I first knew him from his visits to New York, where he spoke of modern superficiality as the sentimental seed of dire cruelties. The former chaplain of the Sorbonne had studied social science there with the worst man in the world, Pol Pot, and he knew the heights and depths of man, as well as the deadly shallows. Even so, he was astonished, as an apostle and anthropologist, that when he raised

a theological question at the dining table of an American
cardinal, an auxiliary bishop sprang to his feet and sang an
Irish song amidst gales of laughter.

I said Mass with him in his residence in Paris shortly
before the 1997 World Youth Day there, which would
gather one million people. The French government had
tried to block the whole event. He said his part of the
Mass in English, which he was trying to perfect for the
great event, and assigned to me the rest in French. After-
wards in the sacristy, he asked, "Where did you learn to
speak our language the way you do?" The pregnant ambiguity of the compliment, or its opposite, was a vintage way
of the French being French.

Many wept on his last visit to the other 39 Immortels
at the Acadamie Française a few months before his death
from cancer. They did not question his place in Paris as a
prince, and more than that. And when he carried the cross
each Good Friday from Notre Dame to Montmartre, no
one doubted that he was perfectly cast to do that from
above. "For if he had not hoped that they that were slain
should rise again, it would have seemed superfluous and
vain to pray for the dead (2 Macc 12:44)."

Erik Von Kuehnelt-Leddihn

❧

It is by way of solid compliment to call Erik von Kuehnelt-Leddihn (1909–1999) a Baroque incarnation, like an enfleshment of Salzburg's *Kollegienkirche*, for the Baroque is an art of overstatement done so elegantly that truth is not distorted. The one glaring understatement I heard from him was, "I dislike specialization"—words baroquely unbaroque in the flamboyance of their diffidence. One of the most florid polymaths I have known spoke eight languages and worked so well in eleven others that sometimes his syntax slid from Baroque into Rococo, to the frustration of editors.

The universities of Vienna and Budapest taught him law civil and canonical, theology, and political science. Sixteen young years after his birth in Vienna, he became an essayist for the *London Spectator* and was not yet twenty-one when he took up residence in Russia as a correspondent for a Hungarian newspaper. Annual research trips took him to the Subarctic and other regions, and that tally eventually added up to seventy-five lands. "Most of these countries I have visited on several occasions: Vietnam, for instance, five times and Northern Ireland recently twice." Utterly contemptuous of a certain breed of superior Europeans, he boasted having visited all fifty United States, and added with an imperial air, "including Puerto Rico and the Canal Zone." These journeys produced journalistic commentary for fifty-one journals in thirteen countries, plus four novels and six volumes of political philosophy. The Austrian aristocrat championed America's Founding Fathers and the Hapsburgs with both fists. Although he would have disdained the term inculturation as a modern vulgarism, he took on the local color wherever he was, but more like a peacock than a chameleon.

The 1930s were testing times for faithful Catholics in Austria when brutalism was crucifying the Baroque. When a people's religion dies, its culture is moribund. As the Nazis annexed his homeland, he left for Washington to teach at Georgetown and, after a second inspection of the Civil War in Spain, he lectured in a few other Catholic colleges on various subjects, including Japanese at Fordham. If he was a dilettante, so was Rubens. Painting, however, was his one blatant mediocrity. He claimed to enjoy much more wielding the brush than the pen and began exhibiting in 1971, but unless you liked a frail attempt at Bosch, his esteem of what he painted was singular, and it was a topic we did not discuss.

My last conversation with the Professor was a year or so before he died, over lunch arranged by his patron and friend William Buckley, who called him the most fascinating man he had ever known. Incapable of gracelessness, our host mortified himself by remaining virtually silent as Erik reviewed with me the chronicles of kaisers and crusades, from the purview of a world trembling on the

brink of an uncivil hell. Not that there was anything disso-
lutely pessimistic about the Professor's extreme conservative arch-liberal monarchist politics, which were essentially
libertarian: "I comes from God, and We from the Devil."
His heroes included Tocqueville, Burckhardt, and Mon-
talembert, and the last non-specialized endeavor of his
closing years was a study of the spiritual problem of Eros
as distinguished from sex. It was a pity that he did not
live to see the papacy of Benedict XVI, who echoed some
of this Eros in his first encyclical. Nor did he witness the
beatification of Emperor Karl, who was the very model of
all he meant a king to be.

When war clouds blew away, the Professor made a home
for fifty years in the Austrian Tyrol, and singing his joyful
Requiem at a gilded altar were grandchildren and great-
grandchildren from the three children born to him by his
wife, Christiane Goss, a Baroque hybrid of Countess and
Doctor of Philosophy. Looking back on three of the cruelest
gaucheries against the human race, two of which he had seen
first-hand, he had decreed with stentorian confidence: "All
forms of totalitarianism, all leftist ideologies, have opposed
individualism, reaching their culmination in the French,
German, and Russian revolutions, and they did this with
the aid of guillotine, gallows, gas chambers, and Gulag."

Henry Hyde

❧

There were two political Henry Hydes, and until the second lived his life's span (1924–2007), no historian would have imagined the *Clarendon Papers* of the mercurial Jacobite (1638–1709) being eclipsed in social importance by a Hyde from Chicago. In his Irish Catholic family, Henry Hyde had virtually no political option: To a Democrat, the Republicans were a bunch of bankers, bloated bondholders, and economic royalists. After combat duty in the Philippines with the Navy in World War II, the Cold War modified his politics and by 1952 he was supporting Eisenhower as deftly as Clarendon had switched royal families, but without the calculation of self-interest.

The Illinois lawyer had Lincolnesque affinities and began to perceive the nation engaged in a cultural war no less vital than the slavery battle. He moved to Congress from his state legislature and eventually chaired the House Judiciary Committee, during which time he was lead House manager for the Clinton impeachment trial for perjury. It was a ticklish business that would have been dismissed as partisan venality, save for the conviction of principles, which he said were "not the ravings of some vast right-wing conspiracy, but a reaffirmation of a set of values that are tarnished and dim these days. . . . " Of more permanent consequence was his Hyde Amendment, which, by prohibiting the federal funding of abortion, has saved countless lives.

As emotive as the abortion question was, he considered its moral and constitutional implications with a lawyerly eye. He told me once in a passing comment that President Bush Sr. had been even more supportive than President Reagan, especially in backing up court nominees. Intelligence legislation actually took more of his time as he headed the House International Relations Committee from 2001 to the year of his death. The empirical spirit that never left him bereft of confrontations with more pliable opportunists moved him to co-author health legislation with a Democrat and break party ranks on arms legislation and military maneuvers in Iraq.

Purgatory came prematurely in scandals fomented to crack his moral stature. He was exonerated of gross negligence charges related to an alleged conflict of interest as a director of a savings and loan bank. More vicious was the demagoguery that tried to intimidate him during the impeachment trial by exposing an extramarital affair from thirty years earlier. The public embarrassment was cruel to him and the memory of his wife who had died six years before the details were advertised by the pharisaic hermeneutic of an Internet magazine. By then, Hyde was so venerable among his peers that even political opponents felt sullied by the tawdry politics. Still, interested agents even shadowed him to Mass in Arlington, Virginia where he was a lector. A private eye copied as evidence that he might be a slave of theocracy, an inscription on a statue

of St. Thomas More in the church: "I die the King's good
servant, but God's first."

It was hard to imagine that the bulky figure walking
on two sticks had played basketball at Georgetown, once
guarding George Mikan in a tournament game and helping
to take the Hoyas to the 1943 Final Four. We were often
on the same platform, and at a meeting of the Jacques
Maritain Society in Princeton he critiqued some things I
had said on television and had forgotten. Somewhere I still
have a video of the father of four children singing to my
own mother on her birthday.

Remembering Douglas MacArthur from combat days,
he appropriated the general's cadences: "When I cross the
river for the last time, my thoughts will be of the House,
the House, the House." Heart surgery prevented him
from receiving in person the Medal of Freedom, and he
died three weeks after the president honored a powerful
defender of life, a leading advocate for a strong national
defense, and an unwavering voice for liberty, democracy,
and free enterprise around the world. The true gentleman
of the House, as the president called him, had said during
the impeachment days that honor is the only thing we get
to take with us to the grave.

Dominic Tang Yee-Ming

❧

Shanghai today is almost unrecognizable from what it looked like in the 1940s, when the young Jesuit priest Dominic Tang Yee-Ming (1908–1995) bicycled with his friend Rev. Ignatius Kung Pin-Mei from parish to parish to hear confessions. He taught English in the Jesuit high school in Shanghai where Kung was the principal and Latin teacher. The native of Hong Kong had entered the novitiate in Spain in 1930 and was ordained in 1941. China became Communist in 1949, and his appointment as apostolic administrator of Canton in 1950 was close to a death sentence. That became clearer when he was consecrated a titular bishop in 1951. His first act was to consult with his friend who had taken on a similar yoke as bishop of Shanghai. His consecrator, the French missionary bishop Gustave Deswaziere, had minced no words: "By accepting the appointment from the Holy See in these difficult times, the new bishop is showing absolute obedience and a spirit of sacrifice."

The government indicted him as the most faithful running-dog of the reactionary Vatican and imprisoned him without trial or conviction of any specific crime on

February 5, 1958. Thus began twenty-two years in prison,
including seven years of solitary confinement. Malnutri-
tion and mental torture were some of the sufferings he
would record in his journal, *How Inscrutable His Ways!*, published in 1987. "I obeyed only the regulations which did
not conflict with the principles of my faith. . . . " There
are many opportunities for practicing virtue in prison.
Bishop Kung would endure similar affliction for thirty-
three years and, like him, Tang contracted cancer and was
sent to Hong Kong upon his release in 1981 in what the
government called an act of leniency. In that same year,
Pope John Paul II elevated Tang to archbishop.

I came to know him in the last years of his life when he
spent his exile visiting Chinese Catholics in Japan, South-
east Asia, Australia, Europe, the United States, and Canada.
A joy to him was celebrating anniversaries with his mentor,
who had been made a cardinal. Our last time together was
in Connecticut at Cardinal Kung's celebration of sixty-five
years in the priesthood. One month later, at 1:40 p.m. on
June 27, he died from pneumonia. Archbishop Tang had
not expected to die first: "Cardinal Kung and I are the
only two bishops from Communist China living in the free
world. The Cardinal is seven years older than I. He cannot
travel easily. I must do the traveling for both of us, to bring
the situation of the persecuted Church to the free world."

When I first met him, I had little knowledge of his
life. We both spoke at a symposium in St. Mary's Seminary in Baltimore. At lunch I was surprised by how he kept
dropping his food. Later I learned that his hands had been
crippled during his prison years. I still reproach myself for
my superciliousness. When he offered Mass in the chapel,

deacons assisted him as he shuffled up the long aisle. After his only pair of shoes had worn out in prison, he had spent the rest of those twenty-two winters barefoot. The Communists had promised to release him at any time, if only he would renounce allegiance to Rome. From the altar he cried out three times to the assembled faculty and seminarians in halting English: "No pope, no Catholic Church!"

When he was dying and apparently unconscious, Cardinal Kung held a crucifix to his lips and he kissed it three times. Archbishop Tang's body was taken to California for temporary burial in the old Mission of Santa Clara, where the local bishop gave permission for a Pontifical Requiem Mass in the old Latin use, provided it be celebrated facing the people. Cardinal Kung's prayers seem to have worked: Shortly before the rites, permission was given for the Mass to be offered facing East. Five years later, His Eminence was buried next to his friend, and both bodies face the horizon in the expectation that the two old men who, in youth, had bicycled together will in a great dawn be buried in their cathedrals of Canton and Shanghai.

Dennis Clinton Graham Heiner

❧

very All Souls Day at the Sanctus I leave it to the Just
Judge to choreograph those assembling around the altar
from the Church Expectant and Triumphant. On the
list now is Dennis Clinton Graham Heiner (1927–2008),
who crossed 38th Street daily for Mass.

Outwardly, Dennis had a coddled childhood in New
York City, and his parents sought the best for him, sending
him to St. Bernard's School, whose establishment aura was
complemented by his parent's devotion to the progressive
principles of John Dewey. Robert Graham Heiner and
Frances Eliot Cassidy were friends of Margaret Sanger and
promoters of her eugenic theory. Their home resonated
with the peaceful intercourse of curious savants from
Planned Parenthood who met to discuss the annihilation
of unfit people, blithe in their assumption that their sort
was not threatened.

Dennis may have misrepresented himself to enlist in
the Navy as a teenager, and so he served in World War II,
if only at the tag end. From there it was Harvard and then
Yale Law School. Mental exhaustion from the war, and
growing interior conflict with his parent's view of creation,

or the lack thereof kept him from ever practicing law. Instead, he pursued medicine at the University of Paris, but never practiced that either.

He had become a Catholic in contradiction of everything his parents understood to be rightly ordered, though he never broke with them in bonds of affection. That only increased his tense nature, and then he met a psychiatrist in the form of a stately Cuban woman, Helena Reina, who left all behind in the Marxist revolution of Castro. They were married for more than fifty years, and all the while I knew them he was her nurse, for she had become blind and nearly comatose. Even toward her end, whenever I brought her the Blessed Sacrament, he sat her under an oil portrait of herself in youth. Not once did I ever hear him speak of her as anything but a blessing, or of her infirmity as anything but a benison, and he seemed never so joyful as when he tried to make her drink through a straw.

I envied his quiet library of the Greek classics and modern apologists up to Ronald Knox, and so I was astonished when bookish Dennis was arrested on December 16, 1999, at the age of seventy-two. The Brooklyn Museum had staged a postmodern exhibition called "Sensation," whose centerpiece was a painting of the Virgin Mary covered with elephant dung and pornographic symbols. Dennis had stepped over a barrier and smeared a tube of white paint over it. The incident won international attention and got the mayor involved, and all heaven broke loose. At his trial, he was his own defense and recited a list of the holy images of the Blessed Mother around the world, concluding by saying that he was answering speech with speech.

The prosecutor demanded probation, community service, and one day of sensitivity training, besides an order of protection forbidding him from entering the Brooklyn Museum. Brooklyn Supreme Court Judge Thomas Farber, a Jew, said that he had expected to hear nothing but hate from the defendant but only heard love. He rejected the prosecutor's request and encouraged Dennis to visit any museum he wanted, albeit without a tube of paint.

He never came to weekly confession or daily communion without a pro-life pin in his lapel, and every Saturday he led the Rosary outside an abortion clinic. He was crossing the street to early Mass when a vehicle struck him and, though he told me he was steady, he died two days later. Months before, he had arranged Masses to be said for Helena, who had died the previous April, and his mother, who had never abjured her eugenics. Helena's Mass was the day before he was buried, and his mother's Mass was one hour after his funeral. A couple of years before his death, I informed him that the notorious painting had been destroyed in a London fire. He expressed no satisfaction, but in his silence one sensed that God's judgments are severe.

Maurice Noël Léon Couve
de Murville

❧

I t seemed that wherever he went he would have been more
at ease somewhere else. Even the tranquility of his childhood, passed in an idyllic part of Surrey, was a Channel
away from the grave of his mother who died during his
infancy in Saint-Germain-en-Leye. His father had brought
the seven-year-old Maurice Noël Léon Couve de Murville
(1929–2007) to England to begin a new life, but the old
life was always backstage; after the youth left school at
Downside and graduated from Cambridge University, he
returned to his homeland and studied for the priesthood
at Saint-Sulpice and the Institut Catholique.

In Paris began a friendship with Jean-Marie Lustiger,
whom he outlived by just three months. The Parisian
intellectual climate in the 1950s had not yet become
soporific, and Couve—as he was universally known—
brought back the enthusiasm of the worker-priest movement and neo-Thomism when he returned to Surrey for
ordination in 1957.

His independent spirit was not happy being a curate
in his first assignment, nor was his pastor happy having
one. Three years later he was moved to Brighton, where

eventually he combined parish work with a chaplaincy at the new University of Sussex. Ever the historian, he took an advanced degree in Assyro-Babylonian studies, and had finished translating a history of the Church in China just before he died. For five years, starting in 1977, he thrived as Catholic chaplain at Cambridge. This was his metier, and the cheerful affability with which he made solid doctrine a benevolent contagion converted and re-converted many, as in the golden years of Ronald Knox at the other place.

The accessibility and wit that undergraduates liked in him contrasted with the intimidating grandeur imputed to him by many fellow priests. Gallican *noblesse* was not entirely an illusion. This scion of an old French Mauritian family was named for his cousin, who was foreign minister and prime minister under Charles de Gaulle. He could be oblivious to the impression he made when using phrases like, "In school, chaps of my class only played cricket." Other clerics may have detected more in his demeanor than was there, but the perception of aloofness hardened when Couve became archbishop of Birmingham in 1982.

His visits to Oxford, which was in his archdiocese, would cause a flurry as he arranged every detail for receptions. Once he decreed that we would have Pimms Cup, assigning me to slice the lemons as he humbly mixed the drinks in the kitchen, while wearing zucchetto and feriola. What friends would have called panache, critics called hauteur, and Couve was not without critics for a noble reason: He was rare among the English bishops in his example of confident evangelical orthodoxy in the mold of John Paul II.

Convert Anglican clergymen and their families found in him an expansive welcome uncommon among many

Catholic prelates who were bewildered by so many who wanted to board their ship, for some of these bishops gave the impression of confusing the Barque of Peter with an unfortunate White Star liner. Meetings of the bishop's conference were not his Nirvana. To the bemusement of men who had made peace with a cynical secularism, he was proud of the Faith as only a really humble man dares be. It was Couve's paradox that he was looked down upon by those who thought him condescending.

Lush acres of his boyhood were not the best training ground for the perfect cultural storm that struck him as archbishop. But the contrast enabled him to see its brutality more clearly than progressivists who treated the Devil like a naughty child. The confluent winds in the storm were secularization supported by the state, theological chaos, and demoralization of the clergy made worse by sexual scandals. The latter was so beyond his comprehension that he admitted to making a muddle of discipline. A bout of cancer let him retire five years before the canonical age of seventy-five, and he lived a dozen more years. Lasting legacies were his promotion of family life, which was being battered—"and aren't we seeing the results of it"— and the creation of the Maryvale Institute as a college for training the laity to be orthodox catechists.

Charles de Gaulle said that the graveyards are full of indispensable men. Like Grand Charles, Grand Maurice knew that he was not indispensable, but as a Christian he knew he was unique.

William F. Buckley Jr.

⚜

Gstaad in Swizerland was where William F. Buckley Jr. (1925–2008) spent winters skiing and writing the novels that he regularly sent me in the vain expectation that I would read them; they were not his best writing, and I do not read novels anyway, as every day in real life is more thrilling than any fiction. His grand *maisonette* on Park Avenue and 73rd Street probably hosted the most lively conversations in the city, everyone gathered in the red library with wife Pat, who stood as tall as her Boldini-like portrait.

But home was Wallack's Point in Stamford. That is where Bill died at his desk, found by his chef Julian, who was one of the pallbearers. Bill really prepared to die when Pat died less than a year earlier; her public memorial tribute in the Metropolitan Museum of Art, surrounded by Egyptian mummy cases, was the first time among friends he could not speak. The yacht *Patito* had been sold some time before, and the harpsichord stood silent in those months, the lid closed, and through the window Long Island Sound looked vastly empty. Echoing his revered Whittaker Chambers, he said he was weary.

As an American boy going to Catholic school in England, he passed an airfield at the moment Chamberlain
waved a piece of paper announcing peace in our time. For
the rest of his life, Buckley fought the devilish conceit that
peace might issue from concordance with evil. He did this
with a tongue that was the pen of a ready writer and was
unusual among men in that he both spoke and wrote well,
writing over fifty books and 6,000 columns, plus filming
1,500 episodes of *Firing Line*, which, lasting thirty-three
years, was the longest-running program with the same
host on television. English was his third language: first
was Spanish, as his father's principal business interests had
been in Mexico, and then his first school was in Paris. His
most formative academy was the home in Sharon, Connecticut, when the family was not wintering in Camden,
South Carolina. At the dinner table, Buckley Sr. ingrained
in all ten children that God, family, and beauty are the core
of life.

While Pat Buckley could make a quarterback tremble
with one fixed stare, she was the object of her husband's
faithful devotion for fifty-six years, in a cosmopolitan
milieu that did not make the sacramentality of marriage a
priority. The Rosary was his favorite daily prayer, reciting
it for all sorts who had asked for help, which did not pre-
clude the material help he often gave to those with problems from shaky mortgages to taxes and tuition. Regular
confession was a norm, and once we stumbled through a
dark church at night so that he might be shriven. Not the
Mass in English, but the Mass in miserable English, made
the Holy Sacrifice an unholy torture, and he made special
efforts to find it in Latin, although his grasp of Cicero

and Plautus was from an admiring distance. Often he ran lines by me for parsing, even once sending a translation by ship radio from the middle of the Atlantic.

It annoyed him to be thought arbitrary in religion. The line attributed to him, *Mater, Si; Magistra, No* was not his, and while he even published in a book his difficulties with some doctrines, he proved Newman's point that a thousand difficulties do not make one doubt. By his own admission, the Lourdes pilgrim never knew one moment of lost faith and was precise in moral obedience, as when he wanted to do exactly the right thing about extraordinary care when Pat was dying.

There were happy anniversaries, such as his eightieth birthday, and my own sixtieth birthday and twenty-fifth ordination anniversary, which he ornamented with his unique rhetoric. His public memorial, a month after a private funeral, opened with the hymnodic verse, "No foes shall stay his might, though he with giants fight. . . . " St. Patrick's Cathedral was filled and overflowing for the Mass, which it was my lot to celebrate and preach, ending with his own words: "What is the greater miracle: the raising of the dead man in Lazarus, or the mere existence of the man who died and of the witnesses who swore to his revival?"

Richmond Lattimore

ᘒ

His Quaker parents had gone to Baoding, then Paot-
ingfu, some eighty miles from Beijing, to teach English for the Chinese government, following the Boxer
Rebellion. Richmond Lattimore was born there in 1906
and was taught by his parents. A sister, Eleanor, later wrote
children's novels about China, and brother Owen became
one of the century's ranking Sinologists, although something of a naif when it came to politics.

After an eclectic education, Owen was a political advi-
sor to Chiang Kai-shek in 1937 and in the heady days of
iron Soviet expansion he became a vague Stalinist, even
defending the Soviet Gulags with the same insouciance as
Eleanor Roosevelt. Senator McCarthy made him a principal
subject, but charges of being a Russian spy were dismissed
after Senate hearings. He lacked the indolence which would
have made his political incompetence harmless and it took a
toll on his academic career, although he was a leading light
at Johns Hopkins. Both the Soviet Union and Red China
took umbrage at his promotion of Mongol culture, which
reached an apogee when Mongolian paleontologists named
a recently unearthed dinosaur after him.

Richmond, always called Dick, kept himself to the
safer climes of ancient Greek studies. The Lattimore family returned to the United States in 1920, and Dick went
to Dartmouth, establishing himself as a well-published poet
before graduating in 1926. He insisted that a translator be a
poet, as in the series of lectures at Johns Hopkins which were
published in 1958 as *The Poetry of Greek Tragedy*. The American
Academy of Poets elected him to membership shortly before
he died on February 6, 1984. After Dartmouth he studied
at Oxford as a Rhodes Scholar, and received his Ph.D. in
1934 from the University of Illinois for a dissertation on
Greek and Egyptian epitaphs. While lecturing all over, his
home base until retirement in 1971 was Bryn Mawr College
as Paul Shorey Professor of Greek. Even while fighting in
World War II as a Navy lieutenant, he wrote on Sappho and
Catullus and translated Homer, Aeschylus, and Virgil for
his book *War and the Poet*. In him exulted the human essence
described in C. S. Lewis's sermon of 1939, "Learning in
War-Time," for Lattimore was in the ranks of those ardent
men who combed their hair at Thermopylae.

Every week, while not a professed Christian, he
attended the church in Rosemont where I was rector, praying in his own way with his wife Alice with whom in 1935
he had begun one of the happiest marriages I have known.
Their simple home was adorned primarily with books and
with Alice, whose unaffected virtues could have adorned
the lintels of Bethlehem or Bethany. One of their two
sons became professor of classics at UCLA, and both were
Dartmouth men, so it was something of a college reunion
on the day Dick's granddaughter Judith became the first
person I ever baptized.

After the monumental translation of *The Odyssey* and even more transporting *Iliad*, he Englished the Four Gospels, the Book of Acts and Epistles, and the Revelation, whose author he did not think was the Apostle John. There was one evangelist he preferred for his elegant Greek, and when recovering in the hospital from surgery he said that his doubts about the Faith had disappeared somewhere in Saint Luke. He announced that he would be baptized at Easter. At the public baptism, with closed eyes and head uplifted, Dick solemnly recited the Creed, whose Greek was his vernacular. He instructed that at his funeral this story be told to all his academic colleagues.

In the Lattimore text of Book 19 of *The Odyssey*, Eurycleia recognizes Odysseus as she bathes him, and the water spills on the floor: "Pain and joy seized her at once, and both eyes filled with tears, and the springing voice was held within her." Having been bathed in another water, Dick kept his first and last Easter, and in one last springing voice his paean to Achilleus became a right epitaph for the professor: "So, even now you have died, you have not lost your name, but always in the sight of all mankind your fame shall be great."

Bent Juel-Jensen

❧

In the Danish town of Odense, the tomb of Saint Canute IV, who had tried to conquer William the Conqueror, has a bullet mark from a clash with Nazi occupiers. Bent Juel-Jansen (1922–2006) fought in the Danish resistance, helping Allied airmen escape, and later served two years in the navy, having been born in that same birthplace of Hans Christian Andersen on the feast of St. Martin of Tours, patron of sufferers from infectious diseases. His father, a teacher, collected books, and this became a lifelong passion in his son, who attended the Cathedral School close by Canute's tomb and completed medical studies in the University of Copenhagen, having established a pen-pal correspondence with Mark Maples, an English boy at Harrow who was killed in an air crash while serving in the Air Fleet Arm.

Juel-Jensen went to England and married his friend's twin sister, Mary. He kept a photograph of her brother in his study, which was filled with rare books, medical tomes, lepidoptery, stuffed birds, stamps, coins, and animal skeletons. Near the end of his life he would edit a Latin study on curiosity cabinets, *Musaeum Clausum*, but none could have been more curious than his own.

Taking two more degrees in Oxford, he studied physiology in New College and pioneered studies in herpes, shingles, and glandular fever, and worked with Sir George Pickering on vascular disease, saving the life of a friend by his diagnosis of fungal septicemia. Oxford created for him the position of University Medical Officer, and as President of the British Student Health Association he set the model for systematic health care in a university which had gone some seven centuries without paying much attention to it. He named a social center for medical students for Sir William Osler of Johns Hopkins and Oxford, physician and bibliophile, and his other hero was also a surgeon and book collector, Sir Geoffrey Keynes. By this time he had an international reputation for knowledge of Elizabethan dramatists and Renaissance incunabula, assembling an unsurpassed collection of Drayton and, just months before dying from the effects of a stroke, purchasing a rare copy of the 1633 quarto of *The Spanish Tragedy* bidding a huge price at auction although he could no longer speak. Having transited from the state church of Denmark to that of England, he continued to collect Danish books about missionaries in Iceland, Greenland, and the colony at Tranquebar in India.

The honorary fellow of the Royal Geographical Society established medical centers in Bhutan and Kenya and accompanied the botanist Oleg Polunin to Ethiopia in 1973. There to his many languages he added Amharic and the Coptic liturgical language, Geez, preserving priestly books and collecting Aksumite coinage dating to the third century. Four hundred of these gold coins were his bequeathal to the Ashmolean Museum. When Hailie Selassie was overthrown, his knowledge of anti-Nazi sabotage techniques served him in fighting the Mengesha regime and succoring refugees. Having fathered one daughter, he adopted the Ethiopian son of Ras Mangashia, governor of Tigray, whose rock-hewn churches he had helped excavate.

In a more peaceful residence back in Oxford, graciously housed in Headington, he was Fellow and Dean of Degrees in St. Cross College, from which on one sunny day in his brilliant convocation gown he led me and a line of graduate students down the curving High Street to the Sheldonian Theatre for matriculation, like a proud hen leading the brood. Juel-Jensen called himself midwife and undertaker to countless students and could be extravagantly kind, despite intimidating flashes of temper which may have inspired his interest in hypertension. I shall take to my grave his voluble rage when correcting my pronunciation of the philosopher about whom I was writing a book: "You cahn't say Kahnt. It is Kant." I stood next to this enemy of tobacco one day in a food shop when, attired in his academicals, he approached a man about to light a cigarette, grabbed the offending object, and ground it into the palm of the stunned man's hand. Music soothed him, and he was patron of the New College choir school, regularly listening in prayerful repose as the choristers voices trembled the sacred vaults built by William of Wykeham. Religion to him was a practical thing, and he rebuilt a church on St. Kilda in the Outer Hebrides while also investigating a pox off the Pembrokeshire coast.

To a list of patrons on a marble tablet in the Bodleaian Library, beginning with the fifteenth-century Humfredus Dux Gloucestriae, is now added Benedictus Juel-Jensen. He would not have needed me to tell him that the present Duke of Gloucester's wife, Birgitte, was born in Odense.

George Edward Lynch

✣

atafi in Mauretania Caesariensi was a town in the western part of modern Algeria, and its chief claim to fame was that it was the birthplace of Marcus Opellius Macrinus who succeeded Caracalla as emperor, albeit for just fourteen months. Because the Berbers there eventually were Islamicized, it was ripe as a defunct diocese to become the Titular See of George Edward Lynch (1917–2003) when he was ordained auxiliary bishop of Raleigh, North Carolina, in 1970. He retired fifteen years later without having had a diocese of his own, save for that vague, arid African abstraction, but to thousands he was a most convincing specimen of apostolic succession as the vibrant DNA of the Faith.

Born in New York, he assumed that he would be a priest there, but soon enough he was recruited as a missionary in North Carolina, which to most New Yorkers in his time was as exotic as Satafi in Mauretania Caeasariensi. The Archdiocese of New York had a surplus of priests and the Diocese of Raleigh had few, and soon after World War II, George Lynch was inviting others to join him as priests where Catholics were rare and often unwelcome.

Although he led opposition to racial segregation prudently and without strife, his work for civil rights did not make Catholicism blend into the cultural fabric. In fifteen years as auxiliary bishop, he was able to see the fruits of his labor in the coalescence of a New South, and in retirement he was vigorous enough to take up a new cause when he returned to live with his sister in New York.

He latched on to the precedent of Thomas Lynch (no relation), one of the signers of the Declaration of Independence, as a model of the men who would "mutually pledge to each other our lives, our fortunes, and our sacred honor." I have a copy of his personal transcript of those words, in handwriting as neat and precise as he was in figure and regimen, tall and white-haired with a gentle manner and soft speech more Carolina than Bronx. Over the years of his pro-life work, he was arrested many times around the United States and abroad, including Russia. The circumstances of his confinement often were harsh, and yet he enjoyed the chance to evangelize men who were imprisoned for less altruistic acts. During a demonstration outside an abortion center in West Hartford, Connecticut, he was severely beaten by policemen who had removed their nameplates and badges.

Gradually all this took a toll on his health, and once during Mass he fainted and returned after resting briefly on a vesting table in the sacristy. From behind the scenes, Cardinal O'Connor approved and encouraged his self-crafted apostolate in the pro-life movement, and when Bishop Lynch died in his sixtieth year of priesthood and thirty-third as bishop, the cardinal privately remarked only half jokingly when the funeral was over that it might not be too soon to start work on his canonization.

It was during his sabbatical in Rome a few years before his retirement that I got to know him, he celebrating Mass and I preaching in the church of our patron San Giorgio in Velabro. At the time I was most conscious that it had been the titular church of Cardinal Newman, but now I also think of it for Bishop Lynch having offered the Holy Sacrifice there.

No one in that church of St. George had to persuade George Lynch that dragons are real. He dueled with them much of his life. In that letter of his that I have here on my desk, he says that "many who have been penalized by heavy fines, long prison terms, and in various other ways" for protesting against abortions could "say and mean" the pledge made by Thomas Lynch of South Carolina and his fifty-five fellow signers in 1776, "and I am willing, come what may, to be numbered among them."

Patrick Peyton

❦

It was astonishing to see thousands thronging the Jai Alai arena in West Palm Beach a few years before the death of Father Patrick Peyton (1909–1992) when I helped him with a Rosary Crusade, but I should have known that by his standard it was an unexceptional number, even smallish. No priest, unless he happened to be a modern pope, has ever addressed such crowds: two million in San Paolo, another two million in Manila, 1.5 million in Rio de Janiero and half a million in San Francisco, not to mention the hundreds of other congresses not much smaller. While he rode the crest of a mini-religious revival after World War II, he slogged on through the chaos after Vatican II when some benighted priests were telling the faithful to toss out their rosaries.

He began as one of nine children in a cottage in the Mayo village of Carracastle. In 2009, the centenary of his birth on January 9 was celebrated with some reverent fanfare. Their pious father consecrated him and his brother Tim to the Sacred Heart before they emigrated to Scranton, Pennsylvania in 1928. Travel for the poor was a thing rare in itself and rarely repeated, so *bon voyage* meant farewell, and Patrick remembered the last sight of his mother waving a handkerchief as his train pulled out of the station. He worked as a sexton in the Scranton cathedral, while his brother worked in a coal mine. Both entered seminary and a year before ordination in the Congregation of the Holy Cross, Patrick fell to what was diagnosed as incurable tuberculosis, and was miraculously cured, in his estimation, by the intercession of Our Lady of the Rosary. The ordination took place at Notre Dame University just as Germany was about to invade the Soviet Union. A year later, his superiors gave him permission to launch a project in Albany, New York for promoting Rosary devotion and family life.

With audacity born of guilelessness, he cajoled celebrities to help. In 1945, as soon as the Mutual Broadcasting Company promised him a half hour of radio time on May 13, he telephoned Bing Crosby who returned the call after shooting a scene for "The Bells of St. Mary's." After Crosby volunteered, he signed up the parents of the five Sullivan brothers who had drowned together when their ship was torpedoed. Add all that to the fact that Truman declared May 13 a day of thanksgiving for the German surrender, and Father Peyton was off and running.

With the advent of television, he easily made the transition with Family Theatre Productions, giving the impression of Kermit of the Muppet Show, arranging guest stars in productions which, refracted later through a more cynical lens, were not always absent of unction or kitsch. It became obligatory in those halcyon Eisenhower years of civic religiosity for Catholics and their friends to do their duty in cameo roles: Grace Kelly, Loretta Yong, Frank Sinatra, Irene Dunne, James Cagney, Margaret O'Brien, Helen Hayes, Maureen O'Hara. And they reached beyond parochial borders:

Lucille Ball, Henry Fonda, Jimmy Stewart, Jack Benny, Shirley Temple, and Ronald Reagan. As an assistant cameraman for a feature with William Shatner, George Lucas got his first film credit, and James Dean made his first credited film appearance. All in all, there were 800 radio programs and eighty-three television specials through 1969.

Father Peyton was Hollywood's ultimate Un-Hollywood personality, but the sophistication of holiness can outwit the worldly, an alembic to disordered culture. When we preached on the same platform, I quickly learned that his art was in his artlessness. I dozed a little during his rambling hour-long discourse, punctuated with those signature phrases, "The family that stays together, prays together," and "A world at prayer is a world at peace." He began with a sentimental word portrait of his father saying the Rosary by the fireside in Mayo and sixty minutes later we were back in the same Mayo cottage. Had he been a prodigy of rhetoric, what he did would be only his, but there was another inspiration at work, and soon his impressive frame seemed hidden behind his Rosary. In an age of celebrity preachers with their own cults, he really meant *"cupio dissolvi."* The requirement of his broadcasting contract that there be no doctrinal apologetic might have resulted in anodyne moralism were it not for his transparency to higher things. In the nineteenth century, Archbishop Ullathorne who resembled Father Peyton in his rough elegance, said of the Rosary: "Many a proud spirit has been brought down by it—many a faddy spirit has been made patient by it. . . . 'The weak things of this world hath God chosen to confound the strong.'"

Eric Lionel Mascall

ature conspired in Eric Lionel Mascall (1905–
1993) to flaunt St. Peter's image of the body as a
collapsible tent (2 Pt 2:13–14)—at least I have not
known such an agile mind in such a clumsy frame. He
once stumbled over himself in the dark, and only his
groan prevented me from stepping on his valuable head.
And he was something of an innocent, too: When I had
an Easter dinner with him in a Manhattan restaurant,
he had no idea why someone was dressed as a rabbit for
the children.

The body served him long, if not athletically, for
he was pleased to have lived only a few years less than
the fifth Earl of Aboyne, who had danced in youth with
Queen Marie Antoinette and in his gray hairs with Queen
Victoria. Born in the golden haze of Edwardian Empire,
Eric lived to theologize about space travel. As the finest
Thomist among the dying breed of High Anglicans, he
was called the greatest living thirteenth-century theologian, but he had been trained as a mathematician and
was prepared for the twenty-first century, consider-
ing the implications of aliens in need of salvation. He

expanded the theory of Aquinas—that any one of the Three Divine Persons could have incarnated on this planet—to speculate:

> There are no conclusive theological reasons for rejecting the notion that, if there are, in some other part or parts of the universe, rational corporeal beings who have sinned and are in need of redemption, for those beings and for their salvation the Son of God has united (or one day will unite) to his divine Person their nature, as he has united it to ours. . . .

Having known him since 1968, our friendship grew when I joined the Oratory of the Good Shepherd, an Anglican version of the French Oratory of de Bérulle. The Cambridge dons who started it after the First World War were solid figures like Father Wilfred, one of the stellar Knox Brothers. Annual retreats in England, I being one of the rare Americans, introduced me to some of the most affable men I have known, perpetuating the spirit of Little Gidding, which had been a model for the life they wanted.

It was a wonder that Eric patiently abided the fraternity of the modernist Alec Vidler, for they were as night and day. Alec, who gradually sank into skepticism as his best friend Malcolm Muggeridge rose to belief, finally allowed that the only article of the Creed he knew to be certain was that Jesus had been crucified under Pontius Pilate. Alec grew a long white beard, which amused the queen when he was a canon of Windsor. He also was Mayor of Rye, having been born there next to Henry James's house. C. S. Lewis was less patient with Alec than Eric was, and found it quite remarkable "that we should have had to wait nearly 2,000 years to be told by a theologian called Vidler that what the Church has always regarded as a miracle was, in fact, a parable."

Eric foresaw the decline of his ecclesial Communion and left me with no doubt that, had he lived, he would have acknowledged the infallibility of the pope. On a retreat at the Catholic abbey at Worth, he bid me spend a whole rainy day with him while the others went on an outing to the Brighton Pavilion: "Little do they know, George, that George IV's *batterie de cuisine* on display is actually that of Wellington." When Elvis Presley died, I spread a rumor that the most unlikely Eric had been a devoted fan, and by evening he asked me, with his unmistakable speech impediment, "Why are all the bwothers condoling with me about Elwis Pwelsey?" He spent a weekend in the lodgings of Professor Ian Macquarrie at his beloved Oxford, under the impression that Mrs. Macquarrie was the housekeeper. Saintly Ian told me that as affectionate evidence that the celibate Eric was not of this world.

Of his voluminous works, my vade mecum was *The Christian Universe*, in which he wrote:

> The faith which the Church has proclaimed through-
> out the ages, embraces and coordinates a wider range
> of human experience, opens up more possibilities of
> human living and offers in the end a deeper and richer
> ecstasy of fulfillment than any alternative way of life
> and thought. . . .

On talent nights during retreats, one of the brethren with a gift for sound effects ritually imitated railroad engines and then, after some weak sherry, Eric would read one of his limericks, which eventually were published. Whenever I have a glass of Sandeman, I mutter the one about an altar boy of Dun Laoghaire who stood on his head for the Kyrie.

Avery Cardinal Dulles

❧

eis van der Rohe's dictum that "God is in the details" fit the moral architecture of Avery Dulles (1918–2008). While his physical architecture was likened to Lincoln, the man was discerned in the details: from his conversion to the Faith when noticing the first spring blossom on a tree, to his intimate regard for all ranks of people, never wasting on professorial dialectic time that could better be spent discussing cookies with a rectory cook. That is not to say that he deified details himself: he could be vague about matters not touching life and death, and he was known to confuse his washing machine with the dishwasher.

My first contact with the Dulles family was with a dead one: my father held John Foster Dulles in high regard and we visited his fresh grave in Arlington. I had no idea that there was a son who, to the confusion of the Presbyterian family, had been ordained a priest three years earlier. Not only a priest, but a Jesuit, very unlike his grandfather who had been a liberal clergyman who dismissed the Virgin Birth and condemned not divorce. The family claimed two secretaries of state before Avery's own father, along with a

Civil War general. Uncle Allen directed the CIA and Aunt Eleanor was in the charge of the Berlin desk at the State Department. His mother did not take very seriously the family's claim to direct descent from Charlemagne, naming her poodle Pepi in honor of Charlemagne's father Pepin.

His literature of twenty-three books and about 800 essays exercised the critical faculties of disparate theological camps, but they all add up in sum: "*sentire cum ecclesia.*" As the Church is the Body of Christ, he took its pulse, confident that something stronger than the gates of Hell is not to be measured by pressure systolic and diastolic. When Benedict XVI was elected, it was as if Dulles had conjured something wonderful with the Holy Spirit, for Ratzinger's "hermeneutic of continuity" was his own ballast against sophistry and pedantry alike. One example was his polite perplexity when a prudential opinion about capital punishment appeared in the new Catechism. Dulles feared that the impression of an abolitionist position against capital punishment, as with just war theory, even motivated by "wise and good" pastoral instincts, would seriously confuse the meaning of intrinsic evil. He predicted that, when the heat of the cultural day cools, the traditional doctrines on these matters will be appreciated better. A friend of mine not given to demonstrative piety, watched Dulles praying the Rosary up and down the corridor before and after he wrote.

One day, a brief remark that I made about a favorite hymn we had both grown up with, albeit from two different sides of the same heretical coin, moved him to write a fine letter which in turn moved me to write a book on the history of many hymns we had long known. For several years we celebrated Easter and Christmas together, and the only help I ever gave him was to stop a Christmas tree with real candles from falling on him. After that I claimed to have saved his life or at least to have saved him from being burned somewhat less than Jesuits of the Tudor period.

Polio, contracted while in the Navy during the Second World War, came back with a vengeance in later years, crippling a leg which he dragged in a heavy brace and robbing his voice whose customary flatness in lectures notoriously contradicted the music of his mind. His speechless patience could be heroic when I, uncharacteristically, had to do all the talking. Muteness became rhetorical elegance when the Pope received him at the Dunwoodie seminary. That blatantly providential encounter prefigured "the two faces of death"—dolorous and triumphant—of which Cardinal Egan eloquently spoke at the funeral, recalling words of his friend's last lecture: "As I become increasingly paralyzed and unable to speak I can identify with the many paralytics and mute persons in the Gospels, grateful for the loving and skillful care I receive and for the hope of everlasting life in Christ."

He promised to dedicate a shrine to Newman in my church, if our mutual hero were beatified. Almost coincident with Dulles's death came a strong report that Newman's beatification was imminent. Perhaps they both now cast their red hats upon the Crystal Sea. Dulles dropped his biretta when John Paul II put it on his head. What "Punch" said of Newman needs little effort of transposition to the Jesuit of Fordham: "'Tis the great and good head that will honor the hat, not the hat that will honor the head."

Richard John Neuhaus

꘏

about twenty-five years ago I had the first of many din-
ners with Richard John Neuhaus (1936–2009), when
he was still a Lutheran. He objected to the term "converting" for a baptized Christian who became Catholic:
rather, such a one "embraced" Catholicism. I demurred,
as I thought I had converted, albeit not from so intensely
dogmatic a confession as Lutheranism but from the pleasant perch of Anglicanism. That same evening, he pointed
out that the heating system in a nearby building was being
converted to gas, to which I replied that he should have said
it was embracing gas. Our friendship was not thwarted, and
I became one of countless people whom he called friends
so frequently in his crucial journal *First Things* that it might
have passed as a convention were it not true. While he was
a formidable debater, he won more friends than arguments
and preferred it that way.

Father Neuhaus did not hide his lamp under a bushel,
and he did not wait passively for lampstands to appear. His
religious conversion, or embrace, came after his change of
politics, putting him in that category of liberals who have
been mugged. In his case, he was not mugged by thugs but

by reality, and so the change in social perspective was in
fact the sensible way he saw to effect the civil rights agenda
and other benevolent causes which had become his public
signature. So he became known as a "public intellectual,"
which is a vague term, and must mean, whatever else it
means, a person who is not shy about his thoughts. Our
friend definitely was public. What some did not understand is that he was not a theologian, however theologically
acute his perceptions were, but he was a social philosopher
and, like Chesterton, influenced religion in his capacity as
a journalist. Chesterton's only lapse into false modesty was
his description of journalism as the art of writing badly.
Neither GKC nor RJN could write badly, and I was not
the only one to start reading *First Things* at the end, for
Father Neuhaus's ruminations were like the prize at the
bottom of the Cracker Jack box which normal children
have always opened upside down. Our age's abandonment
of reason and literacy has left us with a burlesque journalism, and it is poignant that Father Neuhaus's last column
was an explanation of why *The New York Times* is no longer
even worth satirizing.

The decay of public writing is a subject for the public
intellectual who, because of the general corruption of culture, is now perforce a social pathologist. Father Neuhaus
died just before the start of a new presidential administration which he anticipated with foreboding. What he had
hoped for in the green years of his civil rights enthusiasms,
has become its macabre caricature, ushering in a Darwinian
utilitarianism in which life itself will be an arbitrary privilege instead of a right. This is something crueler than the
secularism of the last generation's "Naked Public Square"

and more like Vico's "Barbarism of Reflection" which uses the fine technology and tailoring of the last but lost high culture to impose its inhuman agenda.

Father Neuhaus kept a picture of Martin Luther in his rooms, partly I think to animate remarks from people such as me, but also because he believed that people who thought deeply and powerfully, despite their errors, had more of a way with eternity than the functionaries of lifeless remnant religion, such as the National Council of Churches to whose suburbanized Orwellianism he reacted by forming the Institute on Religion and Democracy. But with the collapse of mainline Protestantism, that was like beating a dead horse. Convinced that there is no longer any reason for Lutheranism, he was resigned to the fact that most Lutherans did not agree, either out of conviction or complacency.

Cardinal O'Connor's mentorship was so generous, ordaining him one year after his Profession of Faith, that Father Neuhaus responded with uncritical loyalty and this perspective tinted his assessment of other prelates. He found the language and music of the revised liturgy "a cause of sorrow" but with filial piety he looked away from the Cardinal's own little ways at the altar. Although he was unconscious in the hospital when I anointed him in his last hour, he may have sensed from a higher plane that I used the Douai translation. Having become a Catholic, he began to realize that the Barque of Peter is also the largest of ocean liners with a manifest vaster than any denomination. Big ships are hard to turn around, harder than Father Neuhaus may have hoped, but he was pragmatic: "What I described in *The Catholic Moment* is not a prophecy but the outline of a possibility. There are no guarantees that my hopes expressed in *The Catholic Moment* will ever be realized." Nonetheless, he was impatient with some of the national documents of the bishops of the United States which sounded like the work of Wodehouse's Madeline Bassett, and he regretted that clerical bureaucracy and the life of the mind are not naturally symbiotic.

It was typical that Father Neuhaus got a book out of his near death ten years before he finally put down his pen, and typical too that in it he did not quote a child's prayer without first sourcing it to the twelfth-century *Enchiridion Leonis*: "Now I lay me down to sleep, I pray thee Lord my soul to keep; if I should die before I wake, I pray thee Lord my soul to take."

Stanley Ladislas Jaki

✥

The first impression really was the lasting one in my instance with the Rev. Stanley Ladislas Jaki (1924–2009). More than twenty years later, I vividly see him sitting me down on the porch of a house in Princeton and telling me that religious freedom was the most important teaching of Vatican II and that, in his view, Pope John Paul II's "Achilles heel" as a philosopher was phenomenology.

Father Jaki was a genius and, as true humility dispenses with modesty, he would not have denied it if someone were rude enough to ask, though he would have thought the question more silly than impolite. Suffering fools gladly was not his charism, nor was debate a genre comfortable to him. More than ruffling feathers, he plucked them, and he could turn callow undergraduates to melted butter when they used non sequiturs.

Like his two surviving brothers, he was a Benedictine of the tenth-century Archabbey of Pannonhalma, where he lived through World War II, being ordained in 1948. After receiving a doctorate in theology in Rome, he came to the United States and taught in Pennsylvania, but that ended when he lost his voice after a tonsillectomy. His speech returned, unforgettably, a few years later, but the voice was raspy and must have been a trial to him. No longer able to teach, he studied at Fordham for a doctorate in physics with Victor Hess, who had received the Nobel Prize in 1936 for his discovery of cosmic rays. Then he founded, with six other Hungarian priests, a priory in Portola Valley, California, where he was bookkeeper from 1957 to 1960. He did further studies at Stanford and Princeton and went on to lecture in universities around the world, publishing some forty books, including his brilliant Gifford Lectures at Edinburgh.

He died in Madrid at the age of eighty-four only a few days after having lectured in Rome as a member of the Pontifical Academy of Science. It distressed some— including Chauncey Stillman, who had endowed it—that he would not take a chair in Roman Catholic studies at Harvard, for they thought Father Jaki would restore it to its original purpose; but he was loyal to Seton Hall, where he was Distinguished University Professor. All this while he was under obedience to the archabbot of Pannonhalma, whose abbey he helped with the proceeds of the largest monetary award in the world, the Templeton Prize.

Father Jaki's great lights were Newman and Chesterton, about whom he wrote books from his unique perspective as a philosopher of science, but his intellectual father was Pierre Duhem, mathematician and physicist. He even wrote a book about Duhem's hobby of painting landscapes. That spectacular French pioneer in thermodynamics and hydrodynamics paved the way for Father Jaki's perception of the essential role of Christianity, and in particular medieval scholastics such as Oresme, in providing the mental and cultural matrix for the development of modern physics.

"Science lives by hope no less than religion." The Duhem-Quine thesis, which posits an alternative to Popper's method of distinguishing science from pseudoscience, was, I am sure, at least in its method of observation, behind Father Jaki's claim that Gödel's incompleteness theorem applies to "theories of everything" in theoretical physics.

Father Jaki was the bane of editors, writing brilliantly in English but with thoughts within thoughts and rambling asides that he refused, with the ferocity of a Hungarian hussar, to have retooled. In one book on which we collaborated, he asked permission to add a "small footnote" to one of my paragraphs. Upon publication, I found myself calling Kant a rank amateur in science and recommending Father Jaki's translation of Kant's "shockingly incompetent" cosmogony. It was by far my most erudite footnote, though I had not written it. He also highly disapproved of Rahner's "Transcendental Thomism," which he called "Aquikantianism," a neologism that I mentioned to my tutor, eventually Archbishop of Canterbury, who was a pole apart from the Benedictine in most matters, but deemed it a brilliant confection.

Father Jaki knelt for a holy hour every day and kept rosaries in his pockets for people to join him in prayer. While only a brave man would challenge points dear to him, I remember Father Jaki on long summer days talking with children as if time did not matter; when, as pianist, he played Chopin and Liszt, he seemed the most docile of men. In electing Newman and Duhem and Chesterton for mental fraternity, he was organizing in subconscious hope what might be a convivium in the heavens of the Savior of Science.

Hugh Dacre Barrett-Lennard

❧

"*Je suis L'Armée Britannique!*" declared Sir Hugh Dacre Barrett-Lennard (1917–2007) to a startled French mayor at the Normandy invasion when he arrived with driver and jeep far behind enemy lines, in the 2nd Batallion, Essex Regiment. His title only came with accession to the baronetcy when he was sixty years old, as the result of a navel (not naval) engagement, but he was mentioned in dispatches in the war and got the rank of captain. He was shot in France and struck in the head by a grenade in Holland but slogged on, having been surprised when he arrived at Paris to find that his orderly had been the waiter fired for spilling soup on one of his dinner guests at the Dorchester Hotel.

Benign singularity in almost all his works seemed to have been inherited along with his title. Shortly before his death in a nursing home, he positively boasted of the amiable ways of his great-grandfather, Sir Thomas, the fourth baronet, who ordered servants to leave dishes of water for the rats in the ancestral home, Belhus Manor, and slyly exploited his position as master of the local hunt to distract his friends from the foxes. The old baronet paid little attention to his clothing and sometimes was tipped by visitors who thought he was the groundskeeper. Sir Hugh's own father, a colonial judge, was not always recollect: Upon returning from his honeymoon he retired to his old bed and recalled that he was no longer a bachelor only when he found a stranger in it.

Although the family line had been Catholic since it started in Kent in the fourteenth century, his mother and he became, by conversion, the only Catholic members of the family since the domestic agitations of Henry VIII. Revisions of the internal revenue code required the sale of Belhus Manor in 1923, along with its verdant park that had been landscaped by Capability Brown, and the family removed to Horsford Manor in Norwich. He absolutely insisted that, on a return visit to the old manor when he was about thirteen years old, his mother and he had been chased down the stairs of a tower by a ghost.

With the war cannons quiet, he began priestly studies in the Beda in Rome, and was ordained in St. John Lateran next to a German soldier he had shot at unfatally in Normandy. Both gave thanks for Father Hugh's bad aim. Back in the London Oratory, admirers saw through a kindly lens that he resembled St. Philip Neri himself in his earnest idiosyncrasies. Then, too, the shade of the fourth baronet was not absent in the priest's cassock, sometimes stained with remnants of breakfast, and unmatched shoes. As confessor to visiting priests like myself, he was perfect reason and charity, and his wide mouth and not undersized ears gave the assurance of generous counsel and attention. He obliged a woman who wanted him to hear her confession on a lawn, but he used a tennis racquet as a confessional screen. A couple of his acolytes as unofficial prison chaplain were doing time for assault and battery, and the regular thurifer was a murderer.

On occasion he gave retreats in the United States. In 1991, in the "Windows on the World" restaurant on top the World Trade Center, he blessed a kosher dinner, celebrating the successful kidney transplant of a cousin who had married a Jewish physician in Brooklyn, along with a Korean surgeon who had removed the old kidney and a Pakistani who had put the new one in. That tower is gone now and so, too, the old family manor, which was demolished in 1957. The family portraits have gone to the daughter of the fifth baronet.

The closest I came to a baronetcy was playing the part of Sir Ruthven Murgatroyd in a Gilbert and Sullivan production of *Ruddigore*, when all the portraits stepped out of their frames in Act II. The baronets of Ruddigore were an odd lot, but all ended happily. I think none could have ended as happily as Father Sir Hugh Dacre Bennett-Lennard, as I imagine him slogging on and announcing to the eternal gates at the end of his life's Act III: "*Je suis L'Armée de Dieu!*"